FUEL

MY FIRE

The characters and events

in this book are fictitious.

Any similarity to real persons,

living or dead is coincidental

and not intended by the author.

" TO ALL THOSE WHO PICK UP THIS BOOK, THANK YOU FOR GIVING MY WORDS A CHANCE"

TABLE OF CONTENTS

1

THE FRESH MARKET

This store is amazing. The aisles were full of stuff that my other store doesn't have. It was an upscale grocery store, called The Fresh Market that just opened yesterday. I couldn't wait to see what they had, so I drove a few miles out of my way to visit it. I parked in a huge parking lot and there were tons of people here. It was in Raleigh, North Carolina, where I moved, about 6 months ago from Connecticut. I got tired of the snow and ice and needed new scenery and new people surrounding me.

I had a basket full of groceries and I headed to the checkout, with all my precooked meals. This was so awesome.   They had Bucatini with Roasted Squash and Pancetta, Pimento Cheese Shrimp and Grits, Seafood Stew with Saffron and Orange, Cider Marinated Beef Tenderloin and Boneless Lamb Loin Roast with Harissa Rice. I was so happy and excited to try something new. I bought a few other things that I needed for the week and checked out. I headed for the exit and went out the double doors that opened automatically for me. I wheeled the carriage a few feet out onto the sidewalk and looked out at the parking lot. Ummm.. This did not look familiar to me. I started looking around at the entrances and exits and headed into the parking lot. I was lost and started to get scared. I couldn't find my car. OMG, This has never happened to me before and it was fucking embarrassing. I could feel people staring at me. It was probably my imagination though.

I walked up and down a few aisles of cars and then I began to really panic. I had a 2022 Blue Nissan Z and it was a bright blue, so it wasn't hard to see. I started looking far away at other aisles to see if I could spot it. I couldn't see it and I felt tears welling up. It's not like I could call one of my brothers or my parents because they still lived in Connecticut. I was alone here. What the fuck should I do? I was NOT calling a cop because it was just too damn embarrassing.

I walked back to the entrance to the store and stood on the sidewalk and a tall handsome man came out with his carriage, glanced at me, smiled and then headed out to the parking lot. I watched him and he walked to the end of the lot, turned around and then came back to the entrance and stood on the sidewalk next to me. He smiled at me and said, "I am so embarrassed. I can't find my car." I snickered a little and said, "Join the crowd. I am so lost and embarrassed and I just want to cry". He looked at me and said, "Oh, don't cry, we will look together ok?" He said, "Watch my carriage for a minute?" I shook my head yes, and he walked into the store and came out with a manager. The manager explained that it happens all the time, because people come in the entrance on the other side of the store and there are two parking lots. He said, "You two are probably parked around the other side of the store". He pointed and then he started walking and said, "Come with me."

I told him how embarrassed I was and the tall guy said the same thing. "This has never ever happened to me before." As we turned the corner, we saw the other parking lot and it looked familiar and I smiled. "Yes, this is the lot I parked in. It looks familiar and that is the door I went in." I started laughing and said, "I don't like this store. Sorry, but it's too confusing." The tall guy said, "Yeah, I pretty much came to check it out myself." I thanked the manager and the tall guy for helping me. The tall guy put his hand out and said, "I'm Billy, you?" I smiled and gave him my hand and said, "Emily, nice to meet you and thanks for helping me." He shook his head and said, "I see my car, do you see yours." I looked down the third aisle of cars and said, "Yup, there it is." He was one aisle over from me, and even with my car.

He put his bags in his trunk and then walked over to me. "Need some help?" I told him I was all set. He said, "Ok, Would you like to have a coffee with me over there?" He pointed to the Dunkin' across the street. I sighed and then thought to myself. This is what I came here for, to meet new people and see new places. "Sure, I could use some caffeine right about now. I will meet you over there." He smiled and walked to his car.

He drove across the street and parked his car and I followed. He got out and was standing by his door waiting for me. I parked and walked up to him and we walked in together and he found a seat. He asked me what I wanted and I told him that I wanted a coffee with cream and sugar. "Do you want food?" I shrugged my shoulders. He came back with my coffee and a Bacon, Egg and Cheese on a toasted Croissant.

It was late morning, around 10:30-11:00 and all I had was coffee, before leaving the house, so this was awesome. I thanked him and said, "So what do you think of the new store, now that you lost your car in their lot?" I laughed a little. He smiled and said, "The store was nice, but I think I will stick to Publix and the Weaver Street Market or Food Lion because they only have one parking lot." His eyes were dancing as he laughed a little too.

He had green eyes, a nice smile with white, white teeth and brown hair, that was on the medium long side. He was so cute. He had a mustache and some stubble on his face.

He was about 6'2 and had a slim build, but not skinny. He looked like he worked out. He looked at me and said, "You aren't from around here, are you?" He had a southern accent and I guess he noticed that I didn't. I said, "No, I'm not, I guess you noticed that I don't have an accent." He said, "Actually, you have a northern accent. New Jersey, New York, Connecticut?" I said, "Connecticut."

We had some conversation, back and forth. He told me he was the oldest of three kids and had two younger sisters, named Elizabeth (Liz) and Sarah. He said he was born here and his parents also still lived here. He said, "My mom (Anna) and my dad (Dan) still live here in town, so we are all together. My sisters live in Raleigh too." I told him that I had 2 older brothers, Jack and Jesse and my mom (Hannah) and my dad (Sam) all lived in Connecticut. He said, "Do you have relatives here or friends?" I told him I made a couple new friends at work, but no relatives.

He asked me where I work and I told him I just got a job at Smith & Kaufman Law Firm as a paralegal and that they were really nice to work for. He raised his eyebrows and said, "I am impressed. I haven't seen you there, although it is a big place." I said, "What do you mean you haven't seen me there? Do you work there?" He smiled and said, "I am a new attorney there. I just started about 2 weeks ago. I get all the crap work because I am new and just out of college, but that's ok. I will work myself up in no time." I smiled at him. "Oh, that's nice that you work there too. It's a really nice place and I was so excited to get that job. I am sure we will cross paths at one point or another. My name is Emily West." He smiled at me and said, "Billy Emerson". I corrected him and said, "Attorney Emerson." He laughed, "Yeah, you are right. It still hasn't sunk in yet."

2

BE CAREFUL BABY

He paused a minute and sipped his coffee and then said, "Have you seen the Chinese Lantern Festival yet? It's really pretty awesome. It starts tonight at 5:30. Wanna go see it with me?" I said, "I never heard of it, but it sounds interesting. Yes, I would love to see it with you."   He continued to describe it to me.

"They have displays that tower up to 30 feet and they even have a 100 yard long Chinese Dragon that is really breathtaking. This year they are having the four seasons of nature and animals in their native environments. You go through the Amazon Jungle and walk into a wonderland with animals, insects, reptiles and exotic trees and illuminated plants. They have a Chinese Live show and we can get our pictures taken with lanterns and they have folk art souvenir booths, plus they have food and drinks."

He took a breath and sipped his coffee and continued. "I went last year and they had giant jellyfish and black spotted cheetahs that were glowing orange and they had green praying mantis' and ladybugs the size of small children. It really was amazing. I think you'll like it." He was a talker for sure and he was excited about this Festival.

He seemed pretty smart and knew a lot about this place. I was excited to see it now.   I told him that I had to get my groceries put away and he asked for my address so he could pick me up. I told him I lived at The Ninety-Nine and I was 2C. He raised his eyebrows and said, "Wow. Ok, Small world, I am 3B." I laughed and said, "Are you kidding me right now?" He smiled and said, "I am not kidding. I live there too." We both got up and he said, "I will meet you around 5? Is that ok?" I smiled and said, "Sure, that sounds good. See ya then. Thanks for Brunch." He said, "Anytime."

I walked out and started thinking. I never saw him before, at work or at my apartment. Of course, both places were oversized and I could have walked right by him, over and over and never saw him. I drove home and put my groceries away and folded up my bags and put them in the drawer. I gathered my dirty clothes from the week and put in a load of laundry. It was nice having my own washer and dryer and not having to lug clothes to a laundromat. I went to sit out on my patio while I waited for the clothes and called my mom.

She picked up and said, "Hey baby, how are things going?" I said, "Hi mom, going good, well except, I went to the new grocery store in town and couldn't find my car when I came out. I was so upset and embarrassed." She started laughing and she said, "I know the feeling, because that happened to me too. OMG." I told her I put my groceries away and I was waiting for my laundry. "Oh, Mom, I met a guy and he is taking me to the Chinese Lantern Festival tonight. It turns out he is an attorney in the same place that I work, he lost his car in the same parking lot, and to top it off, he lives upstairs from me. It all seems to good to be true. He took me for coffee and brunch at Dunkin too." She said, "Ooooh. That sounds like a romance about to happen, but be careful baby, don't get your heart broken. It hurts. Take my word for it."

I asked her if she ever had her heart broken before she met my dad and she said, "Twice and it wasn't fun and hurt like hell and when I met your father, I didn't trust anyone, at that point, so he really had to chase me." She laughed. I felt bad and said, "You never told me mom." She said, "Just be careful baby." We had some more conversation about my dad and brothers and then we hung up.

I went to switch my clothes to the dryer and went in to wipe down my bathroom and then took the vacuum to my bedrooms and living room and also went over the kitchen floor. I had a 2 bedroom apartment and used one bedroom for an office and I had a couch in it with a desk. I was allowed to work from home 2 days a week, which I loved. All my assignments were by email anyway, so it was no big deal. I heard that they were going to try to have a couple of attorneys working from home too and see how it went. I finished folding my clothes and hanging up my tops in the closet and went to take a shower and get ready for my date.

I put my hair up in a ponytail and then wrapped it into a bun, did my makeup and put on a pair of jeans with a nice top and took a hoodie in case it got cool. It was almost 5.

I put a bottle of water in my purse, just in case I needed it. I had a lot of things in my purse, just in case. LOL. He came to my door exactly at 5:00, and smiled at me, when I opened the door. "You look really nice, Em." He was wearing Jeans and a sweatshirt and a pair of boots. He looked really good too. His hair was brushed back and I could tell he put gel in it. He looked about 25-26 years old and I was 23.

I let him in and he was looking around and he told me that his apartment was similar, but he had 3 bedrooms and used one as an office. He had 1 1/2 baths and his patio was a little bigger. He said, "You are so clean. I wish I could say the same about myself. I mean I am clean, just not so neat. I have clothes everywhere and I don't pick up like you." I laughed and said, "Most men are like that. I can't stand living with clothes everywhere and it only takes a few minutes to clean them up."

I laughed at him. I asked him, "Are you ready?" He said, "Yes, Yeah, I'm ready. I can't wait to show you this place. It's amazing. We can eat there if you want, or I can take you somewhere to eat first. It's up to you." I told him we could eat there, and that I liked Chinese Food. He told me that they had all kinds of food, not just Chinese. He walked me to his car and opened the door for me and I got in. We drove to the festival and he parked his car. I made a joke and told him to write down the row so he wouldn't forget it. He laughed, but he _did_ write Row J on our ticket.

It was the most amazing place I have ever seen and everything he explained was better than he said. We saw the transition from daylight to nighttime when the lights came on. I never knew they could make all this stuff from Chinese Lanterns. It was so exquisite and interesting. We walked around for a couple of hours and he was explaining things to me and we even watched how they were made.

We got some Crispy Egg Rolls, some Fried Rice, we got some Nachos and Cheese and then we got a giant soft Pretzel with more

Nacho cheese and later on, we got Cinnamon Sugar Glazed Donut Holes. We got a spiked Hot Chocolate with the donuts and had Pepsi earlier with the egg rolls.

It was a really great night and he held my hand the whole time and he was very affectionate. I put my hoodie on after an hour because it got a little chilly. We continued to walk around and we had so much fun together.

He had a great laugh, that I noticed when we were at Dunkin. It was the kind of laugh that made you laugh. He drew you in with his personality. He was fun, loving, happy go lucky and smart and he made me like him.

He took me home and I asked him if he wanted to come in and have a coffee out on the patio. He accepted and we sat outside for about an hour and continued to talk and sip our coffee and I had a playlist from my phone playing in the background. "You like rock?" I told him that I did and we discussed the groups we liked. He liked a lot of them that I did.

He left around 11:00 and asked me to go to breakfast with him at 9:00 tomorrow morning and I accepted. I liked him, I liked him a lot, but I heard my mom's voice, "Be careful baby." He seemed nice enough, but I still took heed of my mom's warning.

I got up the next morning, showered, dressed, put on some make-up and put my hair up. It was still early, so I went down to the clubhouse/Lounge area. I loved walking around there because the walls were all windows and you could see everything around you. It was beautiful. We also had a built in pool, dog park, game room, a business center, a fitness center and a yoga room. I always walked around the whole place and I became familiar with people that worked there.

When I walked into the Lounge Area, I saw two people sitting in a lounge chair together. Their backs were towards me, so I couldn't see their faces. It was a guy and a woman talking. I stood there for a second, not spying, but it looked like Billy from behind and I wanted to know if it was him. Ok, I was spying. Wouldn't you? They weren't kissing or hugging or anything, but if it was him, what was he doing with her? And who was she? Was it one of his sisters? If it was a sister, why didn't she go up to his apartment? I don't know but this all seemed weird to me. I kept hearing my mom. "Be careful baby." Thanks mom. You made me so fucking paranoid about this guy now.

It's probably nothing and I am making a big deal about it and I don't even know if it's him or not. They both turned around and it was NOT him, and I felt like a fool and just made believe I was walking toward the window and then walked away. This was all my mom's fault. Damn it…

I went back up to my room before I got into any trouble. I was getting ready to make a cup of coffee and my buzzer rang. I answered and it was Billy. He had a smile on his face and I let him in. He kissed me on my cheek. "How you doing this morning?" I shrugged my shoulders and said, "Ehh". He looked at me and said, "What's wrong? Am I too early?" I said, "Oh no, no, it's not you. I was talking to my mom yesterday afternoon and I told her about losing my car and meeting you and she said, 'be careful baby, don't get your heart broken' and that is all I have been thinking about and this morning I went down to the clubhouse and I was walking around and I saw a guy and a girl sitting in a lounge together with their backs toward me and got all paranoid that it was you and another girl. I shouldn't even be telling you this." I laughed a nervous laugh. I paused and said, "I can't believe I just told you this. I'm sorry. See what parents do to your head?"

He laughed and said, "It's ok, at least your honest about it all. I got a bad rap before I even started." He had a belly laugh. He continued. "Just so you know, I am a one woman man. I don't cheat and I won't even entertain the dating thing, unless I am very interested, so… you know I am very interested… and I wouldn't be sitting in a lounge chair with another girl before a date with you." He was still laughing and said, "I can't wait to meet this mom of yours." I laughed and said, "Don't get me wrong. I love my mom, more than life itself, but sometimes, she says stuff to me that sticks in my head and makes me go crazy. Do you know what I mean?" He shook his head no and said, "My mom is pretty cool and just tells me that I know what's right and what's wrong and to do what I think is right. Come on, let's go get some breakfast."

I grabbed my purse and we took off. He put his arm on my shoulders as we walked out to his car. He took me to The Waffle House and we ordered coffee first. I had never been here before and looked over the menu and ordered a bacon, egg and cheese biscuit with a side of hash browns. Billy ordered the All-Star Special, which included 2 eggs, toast, hash browns, bacon and a whole waffle. He told me the hash browns were awesome and that's why I ordered a side. He is gonna make me fat. I can tell already that he is a foodie and loves to eat out. He finished the whole special, but he eats pretty slow. Maybe that is because he talks constantly. LOL. It's interesting talk though and I have never been bored with anything he was telling me.

He smiled at me the whole time he talked to me, and his eyes sparkled at me and he was so charming and interesting. He was a little quirky, in a good way. He was appealing and creative and I liked him.

He talked about his college days and parties and his sisters and their boyfriends and now husbands and that he was excited for them to have kids and he wanted to become an uncle in the worst way.

Then he started talking about his job at the firm and the cases they were giving him and said that his secretary was good for shit. I laughed and said, "Why? Is she not doing her work?" He proceeded to tell me that she is constantly on her phone and she has her headphones in. She doesn't file things in a timely manner and she doesn't ask questions, when she should be. He told me that he doesn't think she knows what she is doing. I asked him if he complained about her and he said, "No, I don't want to get her into trouble or make her lose her job, but if it gets in the way of MY job, I will." I told him that it's his work that she is doing and if she is not doing it, then it will directly reflect on him. "Tell the managing attorney, because if something doesn't get filed, then it <u>will</u> fall on you. I wouldn't worry about her. You need to worry about <u>you</u>." He smiled and said, "You are right, I should and I will, but then I won't have a secretary." I told him that they have to provide him with a secretary and that another secretary in the building will cover for her. "That's the way it works." He said, "Ok then, tomorrow I will complain about her. She will probably get a warning first and maybe she will straighten out." I didn't think so, but I just smiled at him. With this kind of job, there are no warnings. You don't do the work, you don't get paid and you get fired. Of course, it depends on the company, but this was a private firm and not an insurance company, so I think she will get fired. I said, "Keep me posted on that."

We finished up our breakfast and I asked for another cup of coffee and he had one too. We sat for a little while and finished our coffee and then he asked me if I would like to go see the

Raleigh Rose Garden. "Do you like roses? They have every kind of rose there is and it's absolutely beautiful. Wanna go?" I smiled and said, "That sounds wonderful. I fucking love roses." I think I surprised him when I swore, but this is me. Take it or leave it. Maybe he was afraid to swear in front of me, because after I did, he started to swear in front of me.

He took me to the Raleigh Rose Garden and it was absolutely the most beautiful place I ever saw. Rows and rows of gorgeous, delicate blooms in a kaleidoscope of colors and the smell was intoxicatingly breathtaking and enchanting. They were exquisite and the velvet petals were so graceful and majestic. It was decorated so beautifully. We walked and walked and he held my hand the whole way through all the gardens and he squeezed it a few times. He took a couple of selfies with me and the roses behind us.

He kissed my forehead and cheek a few times, but that was all. He said, "I hope you like it here. I thought it would be a pretty place to take you." I told him that I absolutely loved it.

He asked, "Are you hungry for lunch? I know a great place that has southern food. Have you tried anything southern yet?" I told him that I haven't had any southern food down here yet and that I was a little hungry. He put his arm around my shoulder and said, "Let's go." He took me to a place called "Tupelo Honey". We got seated outside on their deck and he said, "Do you trust me to order for you?" I said, "Go ahead. If I don't like it, you can eat it." And I laughed at him. He said, "You can order if you want." I told him I trusted him enough to order for me.

I got up to use the rest room because they had no public restrooms at the Rose Garden and well you know…. I got back to the table and he had ordered Fried Pickles and they were just being delivered. They had a garlic buttermilk coating and there was a ranch dipping sauce. He dipped one and motioned for me to try one. I dipped one, smelled it and then devoured it. Wow, that was awesome. I said, "You can order for me anytime you want. That was fucking outstanding." He smiled and said, "I am glad you liked it. I ordered a

Southern Chicken Bit. It is Fried Chicken with Apple Cider Bacon, Dijonnaise, lettuce and tomato on a Potato Bun. I also took the liberty of ordering you a Mimosa. I hope you like them." I couldn't believe my ears. This guy picked everything I liked. Chicken, Bacon, Mimosa's and Pickles. I looked at him and said, "You did good. I like everything you ordered. Thank you." We had a nice lunch together and he continued to talk and talk, but it was all interesting. He didn't have a boring story in there, anywhere. I was mesmerized by him and I think he knew it, but I also think he was mesmerized by me.

He was making a lot of eye contact with me and me with him. They say that the eyes are the windows to the soul and I believe it. He looked at me the whole time he talked and never looked away and I knew he was comfortable with me. Have you ever seen people talking to you and they are looking away from you, like they can't look you in the eye, for some reason or other? I hate when people do that, because it makes me feel like they have done something behind your back and they feel guilty about it or they are hiding something. It's just my opinion and has no bearing on anything.

Some people just can't look people in the eyes, because it makes them uncomfortable. Some people are just plain ole shy or they have a lack of confidence and that's why they can't do it. I believe it's called Eye Contact Anxiety. So…enough about that…Billy did not have any of this and he made me comfortable.

We spent almost 2 hours at this place, eating and talking. He asked me about all the foods that I liked and disliked, places that I have been, places that I wanted to go, famous people that I met and wanted to meet, movies that I saw and wanted to see, rock groups that I went to see and ones that I wanted to see and just about everything. He picked my brain, as they say, and now he knew so much about me and I did the same and knew all about him.

I was right about him regarding being a Foodie. He said he loved to cook, but he also loved to go to restaurants and try new things and then he would try his hand at making them at home. He wasn't a chef or anything, but said he always wanted to be a good cook.

He told me about a place he wanted to take me for dinner, called 'The Big Easy'. He said it was Cajun inspired and they had awesome food there. "Would you like to join me tonight or are you tired?" I smiled at him and said, "I am not tired and I would love to join you. It sounds enticing and I love Cajun, as long as it's not to spicy." He said, "Just save room for a Beignet." I tilted my head and said, "A what? What is that?" He said, "It's a delicately fried sweet dough. It's served hot and served with powdered sugar. They are to die for. Believe me. Save room." He chuckled a little and his eyes danced and sparkled at me. He said, "You are so friggin cute. You are getting to me Em. I just had to tell you." I blushed and said, "Aww. Thank you Billy. You are getting to me too. I like you a lot. I just have to say thank you for taking me to all these beautiful places and for all the food." He said, "You just let me know, if I become overbearing and you are getting tired of me and I will lay off. The last girlfriend I had, dumped me for being overbearing." I looked at him and narrowed my eyebrows. "Are you kidding me right now? Overbearing? OMG. No, I don't think that at all." He smiled at me and said, "Oh good. But please, please let me know if I need to shut up or let up and I will, because I really like you." I assured him that if I thought he was being overbearing I would let him know and he seemed relieved.

He said, "I know we just ate, so do you want to have a late supper tonight, like 7?" I told him, that would be perfect, because I was really full and it was 2:30.

He said, "Do you want to go home and rest till we go out or do you just wanna hang with me. I mean, I am not going to do anything this afternoon, unless you can think of a place to go." I laughed a little and said, "You can drop me off home and I can freshen up and change for dinner and rest a little, if that's ok."

3

SICK DAY

He said, "Sure. Hey, do you think you could take tomorrow off from work? I wanted to take you to the State Farmers Market, but it's kind of a whole day walker. They are having their craft fair right now and there are tons of vendors, Christmas trees, a cow to take pictures with, pumpkins, candles, flowers, cakes, pies and pastry, bread and rolls, plus they have their market with all fresh vegetables and of course, Food. If you are interested of course." My eyes lit up, because I loved stuff like that and I said, "I will certainly try to take a day off. I haven't taken a day off yet, and I don't know what's involved, unless I just call in sick." He laughed and said, "Ok, we will both take a sick day then." I was excited to go there. I said, "Is it in Raleigh? How come I didn't hear about this place. I love that stuff." He said, "Yeah, it's in Raleigh and it's there all year long, but right now the craft fair is there and they have tons and tons of vendors and I think Santa may be there. There are only a few days left and it ends next weekend. I like to go

there for fresh veggies and stuff. Wait till you
see it. It's crazy." I said, "Oooh, I can't wait till
tomorrow." I think he saw how excited I was
and said, "You may have to take 2 sick days."
He laughed. I told him I had a lot of sick days
and vacation days.

He drove me home and I was a little tired after
all the walking and eating and talking. I got in
my sweats, set my timer for 2 hours and laid
down on my couch. The timer was just in case
I fell asleep. Ha-ha, yeah right. Just in case. I
was out like a light and it's a good thing I set
the timer.   I slept for almost the full 2 hours. I
never take a nap, but now that I was out and
about and getting all this fresh air, I was tired.
I wonder if I should text/call my manager now
or wait till morning? I should wait till morning
so they won't think I am faking. Either way, I
_am_ faking it. I ended up texting her now and
saying that my stomach was killing me and I
was having some issues and not sure if I was
going to make it tomorrow. She texted me
right back and told me to stay home tomorrow
and I thanked her.

I hope I didn't jinx myself. We all know how that goes. Hopefully, I don't see anyone from the office tomorrow at the market. Well, if I do, they either called in sick too or took a vacation day.

I got up, grabbed a bottle of water and downed half of it and put it back in the fridge. I went in to shower and then confronted my closet to see what I was going to wear for dinner. I wonder what kind of dress code it was? I am going to google this place and see.

It says casual, so I think a nice pair of black slacks and a pretty top. Something I would wear to work should be fine. Some people said they wore jeans but I didn't want to do that, because this was a date too and they always say, 'dress to impress'. I don't think I had to do much impressing, but I wanted to anyway. I picked a pretty pink top with long sleeves and a pretty black necklace. I pulled my hair back and did a French braid, which took me forever doing it in the mirror until I got low enough to bring my hair to the front to see what I was doing. It came out pretty good, if I do say so myself. I pulled out some pieces to make it a little pouffy and sprayed it to stay in place. I pulled out a few pieces to frame my face too. I put on some silver hoops and a couple of silver bracelets. Now for the makeup and I was going to put on some extra liner and be a little fancy tonight. I finished getting ready and slid into my black boots, grabbed my black purse and put a few things in it and I was ready. I pulled a black dress jacket out of my closet and hung it on the chair.

I looked at my phone for the time and it was 7:10. Hmm.. He was late and he is usually very punctual. I will wait another 10 minutes and if he doesn't come, I will go up to his apartment. I waited 10 more minutes and he still wasn't here. I locked up and took my keys and walked up to 3C and knocked. No answer… I knocked 3 more times and no answer…. I didn't have his cell number and he didn't have mine because we never thought about it. He wasn't home. Did I get the time right? Did he say 7:30? I walked back down to my place and he was standing at my door. I sighed and said, "You scared me. I went up to your place and thought something happened to you. Did I get the time wrong?" He started apologizing. "No, it was supposed to be 7 and this is all my fault. I am so sorry. I left my place at 6:30 to go get you a bouquet of flowers down the street. Did you hear the sirens? There was an accident and I got caught in all the traffic and I then realized that we don't have each others cell numbers, so I couldn't even text you to let you know I would be late."

He handed me the flowers and he looked like he did something bad and he was so sorry that he made me wait. I reached up and kissed his cheek. "Thank you for these. They are beautiful." They were roses of all different colors. I opened my door and we walked in. I put the flowers in a vase and put them on my kitchen table. He kept apologizing for being late and I told him it was fine and that he was forgiven.

He said, "I think we should wait a little bit before heading out because they still didn't clear the accident." I shook my head and said it was fine. He turned me to him and said, "You look stunning Em." I blushed and said, "Thanks Billy." He was wearing black dress pants and a light, light lavender dress shirt. It looked so nice on him and I told him that he was handsome in it. He was still facing me and he bent down and kissed me on the lips, just lips, but OMG, his lips were on fucking fire, or maybe mine were, or maybe it was both of us starting a fire. All I know, was that fire burned all night and he kept the flames going. He was adding fuel to that fire every chance he got.

We went to The Big Easy and he had a table reserved for 7:30, which we missed, but they said we were fine and he explained the accident. They didn't care about the accident, just that we showed up. He ordered a bottle of Del Poggio Pinot Grigio to start things going. Then he said, "How are you at trying new things? I promise you that you will like it." I said, "I am in, go for it." He said, "You are fun to be with, I like you a lot." He ordered Alligator Bites, deep fried and served with spicy mustard. I tried it and I wasn't afraid at all. I dipped it in the mustard and took a bite.

It was delicious. He smiled and said, "You like?" I said, "Yes, I like." He laughed and topped my wine off. I ordered Salmon Lafayette. It was grilled Salmon with brown sugar and a cajun rub and for my two sides, I got Fried Spinach and Sweet Potato Fries. Billy got a half rack of the Big Easy Ribs, slathered in BBQ sauce, with macaroni and cheese and onion rings.

There was so much food on our table and it was all delicious. He made me try his ribs and I let him try my Salmon and we ate each others French fries and onion rings and he put a forkful of Mac and cheese in my mouth before I could refuse it. God, I enjoyed his company so much. So much so, that when he wasn't around, I missed him. What day was this? Day 2?

We had a really good time at this restaurant and all the food was awesome. We were both too full for dessert, but he asked me if I wanted to order some Beignets to go and that maybe we could eat them later with coffee. He said, "They are really good hot, so you should try at least one, before we leave." I agreed, so he put in an order and told the waitress that we wanted to eat one here and take the rest home. She was such a nice lady. She brought us each one Beignet on a plate and then our to-go box and she didn't charge him for the 2 we ate there. He gave her extra in her tip anyway. We finished the bottle of wine in the 2 hours we were there.

It was 10 p.m. and I think this is the latest dinner I ever ate, but it was so much fun with him. As we walked to the car, he fueled the fire again with his hot lips and he did so a few more times in the car. He drove back to The Ninety-Nine and we ended up at my place. I was still very full from dinner and didn't want coffee or dessert.

I suggested a walk around the building downstairs and he looked at me surprised. "You walk around here alone at night?" I told him that I only usually walk in the morning or afternoon, but never at night. He said, "Oh ok, don't ever do the walk at night by yourself. I will go with you, whenever you want to go at night." I told him that I only suggested it because he was here with me and I needed to walk off some food. He laughed and said, "Ah ok, I get it, but please don't do it at night ok?" I told him it never crossed my mind. I took my keys and we locked up and started our walk around the building. We took the elevator down to the main level and there were actually a lot of couples walking around. There were people in the lounge and the game room and it looked like some kind of party going on.

It was a pretty busy place at night. I think Billy was surprised too and said, "Shit, this place is packed at night. I never came down at night either." He was holding my hand and fueling the fire all during our walk. We walked around the perimeter of the building and went into every single room to see what was going on. There was a Batchelor's party happening in the lounge area and a drinking party in the bar area and there were people in the Yoga room, but not doing Yoga. LOL. There were people in the game room and the whole place was filled. We walked outside and walked around the outside of the building and then walked back in and walked up the stairs to my place.

We were gone about an hour and then I made some coffee and we each had another Beignet. They really were delicious, but we were both still very full. He helped me clean up and we sat on the couch, where he fueled the fire even more and started using his tongue. This guy was moving a little fast, but I was enjoying it. As long as it didn't get out of hand, I was ok. It was midnight and he said he had to get going and that he would pick me up around 9 for breakfast and then we would head over to the State Farm Market. I told him that I called in sick and reminded him to do the same. He said, "I called in sick earlier with a stomach issue." I told him I used the same excuse and we both laughed. He kissed me one more time before he left and I thanked him for an awesome day.

I set my alarm for 8:00. I got up and showered and dressed and got ready for breakfast. It felt funny not getting ready for work, but I really needed a day off. This was my first one in 5 months. Billy was right on time at 9:00 a.m. and as soon as he came in the door, he started fueling my fire. Then he walked to my kitchen table, put his phone down and said, "I still don't have your cell number and you don't have mine and this is important to have if we are dating. Right?" I smiled at him and said, "Absolutely." I gave him mine and he gave me his and we added them to our phones. My phone went off and I looked at it and it was Billy. He texted me and said, "I am looking forward to spending the day with you." I laughed and wrote back, "Ditto Dude." He laughed and said, "You ready?" I grabbed my purse and said, "Let's go. I am excited for today."

He took me to a place called 'The Flying Biscuit Cafe'. It was like no other breakfast place I have ever seen and the food on the menu, made you want to order all of it. I ordered something called 'Strawberry Cheesecake Stuffed French Toast' It was two thick slices of Challah bread dipped in their signature batter, grilled, stuffed with sweet cream cheese and topped with raspberry sauce, honey creme anglaise, fresh strawberries and powdered sugar and it was served with creamy dreamy grits. All I can say is Holy Fucking Shit. This was the best breakfast I ever had. Billy ordered the 'Stuffed French Toast Breakfast, which was two thick slices of Challah bread dipped in their signature batter, grilled, stuffed with sweet cream cheese and topped with raspberry sauce, honey creme anglaise, fresh strawberries and powdered sugar and served with two eggs, two chicken sage sausage patties and the grits. This place was outstanding. The food and the ambience, made this place, not to mention the name of it. Can you tell I was impressed? I took a selfie with Billy outside, before we went in and then a picture of the food we ordered and sent it to my mom.

We took off for the State Farmers Market and we started walking around and we walked and walked and saw each and every vendor and we looked at everything and Billy bought me all kinds of things. I had to be careful about what I said because if I said I liked something, he bought it and I didn't want him to spend all his money on me. We walked for hours upon hours and saw all the homemade crafts and candles and flowers and he bought a carrot cake and homemade breads and we went to the actual market and we both bought fresh veggies and went to the deli and bought specialty foods and we had our picture taken with the cow and then again with Santa. We sat at a table with an umbrella and he fueled the fire and let me tell you how hot this fire got. No, I can't tell you…It was rip roaring hot…

We sat on a bench and we were rearranging all the stuff we bought and putting things together into just a couple of bags because we had so much stuff. We still hadn't seen everything, so I suggested that we take what we bought back to the car and go back empty handed. He agreed and said he had a cooler in his trunk with ice so we could put some stuff in there. We took a walk back to the car and arranged stuff inside the cooler and put the rest of the bags around the cooler. He spent tons of money and so did I, but this place was worth it. I loved it and I told him I did.

We went back in and hit the bakery again. He said he wanted to get more sour dough bread and Italian bread and put it in his freezer and I did the same. I bought some hard rolls with poppy seeds for sandwiches. They would go in my freezer too. He told me that the Market Bakery was always here, just not the vendors.

We went to a soup vendor and the soups were all packed in little containers and I bought a bunch of those to take to work. Just pop them in the microwave and you had a lunch. Billy bought a few too. He told me that he thought that at Christmas time, which was right around the corner, there would be another craft fair, or maybe this was it. He wasn't sure, but he said they had Christmas Trees and he would come back to get one and he offered to get one for me too and carry it up for me. I told him I had a small fake tree, but thanked him for the offer.

"It's just cleaner and easier for me." We went to another vendor that was selling Christmas Tree ornaments and they would also make personalized ones for you. Billy bought something as I was looking at what they had. We moved on to get a snow cone and a hotdog and hit a vendor that was selling freeze dried candy and treats and then on to a place that had concert T-Shirts and then another place that had charcuterie boards and kitchen gadgets, then jewelry and perfume and Billy bought me a perfume and the last place was a Jerky, Jam, Jelly and Peanuts place and we each bought some jam and jerky. This place was magnificent and I had the best time with him and I didn't want the day to end.

We gathered our bags and walked back to the car and I told him that I had such a good time and I didn't want the day to end. He said, "It doesn't have to. Come up to my apartment and I will cook you up some dinner. What do you say?" I looked up at him and said, "I say Yes."

He drove back to The Ninety Nine and we carried all the bags up. I dropped my bags off and put the refrigerated stuff away and left the rest in the bags on the kitchen table. Then we went up to his place. It was all picked up and he smiled at me and said, "I picked it up. It really did only take a few minutes." I helped him put his stuff in the fridge and he put the other bags in the bedroom. He took a bag of shrimp out of the freezer and put it in a pan with water. He took out garlic, linguine, butter, white wine and seasoned bread crumbs. He whipped up Shrimp Scampi with Linguine in a matter of 30 minutes and it was fucking delicious. I kept glancing at him and every time I did, he was looking at me. I said, "Wow, this is so friggin good Billy. You really are a good cook." He had the biggest smile on his face. He said, "I'm glad you like it. That makes me happy." He even made a couple slices of garlic bread from the bread he got at the Market Bakery and we each had a coke. I cleared the table and rinsed the dishes for the dishwasher and helped him clean up. He washed the two pans and I dried them. We sat on the couch for an hour and he was adding fuel to the fire the whole time. I told him I had to get going, but it was the best day ever and I thanked him. He walked me down to my apartment, even though I told him I would be fine. He said, "No, I will never let you walk the halls at night by yourself." We kissed before I went in for the night.

4

BACK TO WORK

The next morning I got up, showered, dressed for work, grabbed a chicken soup from the fridge, made myself a couple scrambled eggs and a piece of toast for breakfast and I was out the door. I walked in and looked around, but I didn't see Billy and continued to my office. I turned on my computer and checked my emails and there were a ton of them, so I put my soup in the fridge and marked it with my name. I got to work, answering emails and then got going on typing stuff for the court. I had two days of emails to catch up on, but it was worth it. I enjoyed the hell out of yesterday. Charlene peeked in to say hi. "Hope you are feeling better Em." I said, "Yes, thanks for asking. I am better today. While you are here, can you tell me what I have to do to ask for a day off? I have vacation time piling up and I was thinking about using some of it."

She smiled and said, "Just send me an email and request the days off that you want and I will approve them, as long as the other paralegals are not taking the same days." I smiled and said, "Ok, thanks Charlene. I don't know what days I want yet, but I will let you know. I was thinking about it yesterday." Charlene was not a paralegal or my boss, but she kept track of timekeeping and I reported to her and so did the other paralegals. I really don't know what her title was and I think she only worked part-time because I didn't see her all the time.

I worked for about an hour and then my friend Olivia knocked at my door and said, "Hey Girl, you missed it yesterday." She came in and closed the door. I looked up and said, "Hey, how are you? What did I miss?" She said, "There is a new attorney here and his secretary got fired yesterday because they were monitoring her work, and apparently there was nothing done. He called in sick yesterday and she did absolutely nothing." I looked up at her horrified. "OMG. Really? Why would she do nothing? Now what?" She said, "I don't know.

Apparently, she had her headphones on and she was making believe that she was typing, but she was playing a game on her phone and Attorney Smith caught her and she was fired on the spot. I guess someone will cover for him and they will hire a new secretary. I hope they ask me to cover, he is a cutie. Did you see him yet?" I smiled at her and said, "Yes, I did see him and I went out with him this weekend, but please don't say anything to anyone. I didn't meet him here though. I met him in the parking lot at the new store that opened. Neither of us could find our cars in the parking lot." She had a surprised look on her face and said, "Oh, I know what store you are talking about, because I lost my car there too, on Friday night, when they opened. Don't feel bad. You lucky son-of a-bitch. He is a cutie pie. I wish you luck and maybe they will ask you to cover for him. That would be good. And don't worry, your secret is safe with me." She was out the door and said, "Good Luck."

My office phone was ringing. I answered "Smith and Kaufman, Emily speaking, how can

I help you." It was Attorney Kaufman. "Emily, this is Attorney Kaufman, can I see you in my office? I have something to ask you" I told him that I could come down now and he was pleased. I hung up and walked down to his office. I knocked and he asked me to come in and close the door. I walked in and said, "Good Morning". He said, "Good Morning. Emily, I have to ask you a favor and I know you are extremely busy, but your expertise is needed." I smiled at him and said, "What can I do for you?" He said, "We fired Denise yesterday. I am not sure if you knew her, but she was the secretary for Attorney Emerson on the other side of the office. I wanted to ask you if you could possibly cover for him until we hire someone for him. I am hoping it will only be a few weeks. I know you have a lot on your plate, so if you don't feel that you can handle it, I will understand." I looked at him and said, "I did not know Denise, but I am going to be completely honest with you. I met Attorney Emerson on Saturday at the New Market store and we went out on a date Saturday and Sunday and we are kind of seeing each other.

If you don't care about that, then I can cover for him. We can keep it totally professional, if you don't mind. I will have a full plate, but I think I can handle it and I can always delegate a job to someone else that I know can handle it." He smiled at me and said, "As long as it is kept professional, I know nothing. Can you start today?" I smiled at him and said, "I was out sick yesterday and I have two days of emails to catch up on, but I will delegate some of it to Olivia and some to Evelyn, just so you know who will be doing the work. He said, "Sure thing. Please let me know what work you are delegating and who you are sending it to. This works for me." I started walking out and said, "I'm on it."

I got back to my office and sent some work out to Evelyn and Olivia with an explanation, and sent an email to Attorney Kaufman, letting him know what and who I delegated the work to. I also sent an email to all of my attorneys and let them know that I would be covering for Attorney Emerson as a secretary for the next few weeks and to please ask Attorney Kaufman, what work should come to me. I picked up some of my belongings, locked my office and headed to the other side of the office and found my new desk. Billy was sitting in his office on the phone and he glanced up when he saw movement outside his door. That is where my desk was. I settled in and put my purse in the drawer and signed into the computer. He had sent me a few emails already, so I got right on it. I typed a Motion to Transfer and sent it back to him for his approval and then I e-filed it with the court. I typed a bunch of motions and e-filed them and then got busy with Noticing Depositions, putting them in his calendar and typing the Notices and emailed them to all attorneys and to the court reporter. I completed all his emails and then started in on my paralegal work. I got through half of what I had left after delegating my work.

It was lunchtime. I signed off my computer and took off for the lunch room. I warmed up my soup and grabbed my sandwich and found a seat. Olivia was sitting there eating and I thanked her for helping me with my work. She didn't look too happy and I apologized. "I hope you aren't too upset with me, but I had to delegate some of my work. I gave most of it to

Evelyn. I had no choice. She glanced up at me and said, "No problem, I will get it done."

She didn't talk to me like she always did at lunch. Oh well, tough shit. I did what I had to do and I was told to do it. Maybe she thought she had something on me because I told her I was dating Billy? That's why I made sure I told Attorney Kaufman. I wanted no secrets. NONE. I wanted everything out in the open and I wanted to be honest about it because if I wasn't, it could come back and bite me in the ass.

I finished my lunch and went to take my lunch walk. I did it everyday because I sit almost all day and needed some exercise. Usually, Olivia went with me, but she made no effort and I didn't ask. Fuck her. She obviously was not a team player. Lunch was over and I went back to my desk.

Billy was on the phone all morning, talking to clients and I haven't even talked to him yet. I checked my emails and he sent me 10 more, so I got to work. I typed up motions and e-filed with the court. I called Attorneys and court reporters to confirm depositions for tomorrow. I confirmed a pretrial and meeting with a Judge tomorrow morning and sent him an email, letting him know that the pretrial was going forward but the meeting with the Judge was cancelled and rescheduled for Friday morning and it was on his calendar. He had a deposition at 2:00 p.m. that was confirmed and it was taking place here in this office in Conference Room B. I marked the conference room calendar as confirmed for 2:00 p.m.

I finished his emails and typed up all his motions. I answered the phone a few times. If the receptionist is on a phone call, the phone will rollover to a secretary and we are supposed to answer it. I went back to my paralegal work and continued typing up some motions for my other attorneys and finished all my paralegal work and no more jobs were coming in. I emailed Attorney Kaufman and told him that my paralegal work was caught up and I wasn't getting anymore assignments and he emailed me back and said he assigned Olivia and Evelyn my attorneys for the time being and he thanked me for being a Team

Player. That was a big thing in this office.
They even had meetings about it.   A Team
Player was someone that covered for
someone in their time of need, no matter what
the circumstances were and did not complain
about it.

Billy was finally off the phone and he came out
to say hi to me. "I see that they assigned you
to me. They fired Denise yesterday for not
doing anything but playing games on her
phone. Is this ok for you? Will you get backed
up on your other work?" I told him it was all
worked out and that my work was delegated
to the other two paralegals. I told him that
Olivia was bent out of shape over it, but tough
shit. He said, "I am happy that you are my
secretary. I told Attorney Kaufman that you
were my girlfriend and he didn't care and just
thanked me for being honest and asked me to
be professional." I laughed and said, "I told
him too. I wanted to be honest about it." He
just nodded his head and said, "Good, I'm
glad you did it too." I told him his work was all
done, so keep sending what he needed done.

He looked at me and said, "I sent you about 20 emails, so get to work." I laughed and said, "Those 20 emails are done. You get to work." He was shocked. "Really?" I nodded yes. He said, "Holy Shit. Wow, you sure you don't want this job permanently?" I said, "No, I don't. Paralegals make a lot more money than a secretary." He asked me if I was getting a cut in pay and I said, "I hope not. I don't think they can do that."

He turned around to go back into his office and then stopped and turned around. "Wanna go to dinner with me tonight?" I smiled and said, "Sure do". He smiled and went in his office. He sent me more emails with work to do and I kept up with him. I did his mail and added appointments to his calendar and pulled his files for the next day.

We worked until 5:30 and then I signed off and I went home. He left a few minutes after me. He texted me and said, "You don't have to change clothes, we can go like we are." I sent him a checkmark and he asked me if I was ready. He was at my door before I could answer.

He took me to a place called Seasons 52. This place was fancy and kind of expensive. I ordered the Lump Crab Cake and Billy got the Lump Crab and Shrimp Stuffed Mushrooms for starters. Billy ordered the Filet Mignon and Maine Lobster Tail and I ordered the Brick-Oven Gnocchi. The food here was so outstanding. Billy kept talking about their desserts and saying how they were served in a glass, but I didn't understand what he was talking about, until I saw a tray of them being delivered to the table next to us. He told me to try the Raspberry Chocolate Chip Cannoli. The raspberries and some kind of cream were in the bottom of the glass and a mini chocolate chip cannoli was stuck down the middle. He ordered 2 of them with coffee. OMG Fucking deliciousness. I said, "How did you find all these awesome restaurants?" He said, "I have lived here all my life Em, and a lot of them, my parents took us to. I try all of them and go back to the ones I like."

He paid the bill and tipped the waiter and got up and took my hand and we walked outside.

He stopped to add some fuel to start a fire and I added some fuel too. It wasn't just lips anymore and he was really getting into it. We got into the car and he said, "Would you like to go to dinner at my parents house this Sunday? They usually have dinner every Sunday at their house and everyone comes and we all bring something. She didn't have it this past weekend because she had a cold and didn't feel like cooking." I looked at him and said, "I would love to meet your family. Let me know what I can bring." He said, "You don't have to bring anything, but I will." I said, "I want to bring something. Can I bring a dessert?" He smiled and said, "Sure, bring a dessert." I knew exactly what I was going to bring.

Everyone like's ice cream, so I was going to make a snickers ice cream cake with caramel and chocolate over the top and in the middle.

Billy told me that the whole family loves chocolate and I remembered that, so this would be perfect. I will get her a bouquet of flowers too. Do you think that is too much? It hasn't even been a week that I have known him, although it seems longer. I am actually shocked that he asked me to meet his family already. I will just go with the flow and meet them.

5

TEAM PLAYER

We worked all week together and all his work was up to date before we left on Friday afternoon. I even took some stuff from Evelyn who actually got the bulk of all my work. She was happy that I was helping out. Attorney Kaufman saw me in her office and came in to find out what was going on. I told him I was caught up and was here to get some stuff from her to help out. He smiled at me and just said, "Awesome".

On Sunday, I went to meet Billy's family and they were so nice to me and they loved my ice cream cake and Billy talked me out of buying his mom flowers. He said, "She is not a big fan of flowers." His sisters and their husbands treated me like I was family right from the beginning. His mom and dad kept calling me honey, so I think they liked me, but his mom kept looking at me out of the corner of her eye.

I helped clean up dinner dishes and even dried pots and pans and I told her that dinner was delicious. She made a prime rib dinner with all the trimmings. I think his sisters brought some of those trimmings.

I worked with Billy for a month and then the secretary that they hired was starting and they asked me to walk her through everything and show her what to do every day and how to use the computer.   I did that for another week and I left her and told her if she had <u>any</u> questions that she could reach out to me or another secretary or even Attorney Emerson. I took all my work back from Evelyn and then went to Olivia and told her I was taking my work back from her. She was so nasty to me and she said she would forward everything back to me.

I went into my office and opened my emails and I saw two of them from a month ago that I had forwarded to Olivia and asked her to do. She didn't do them? What the fuck? I sent an email to Attorney Kaufman and asked if he would come in so I could talk to him. I didn't give a shit who this hurt. This would eventually come back to bite me in the ass. I told him that I asked Olivia for the work that was forwarded to her and I would take care of it and with those emails, she sent back two that I gave her a month ago. I told him about the attitude I received. I told him that I am not a trouble maker, but this was supposed to be my work and I didn't want to get in trouble for it and I had a feeling she did it on purpose. He shook his head and then went to her office and brought her to my office. She was fucking scared and she knew why she was here. Attorney Kaufman asked her why she didn't do what I forwarded her a month ago and she said, "I uh, I don't know, I must have missed it." He said, "You didn't miss it when you sent it back to her though. I don't like what's going on here Olivia. You are supposed to be a Team Player and we all help each other. I won't put up with this in my office. I don't like this at all. I will give you a warning this time, but don't let me catch you ignoring work that was delegated to you by someone else. She looked at him and said, "Well then, you probably won't like that Emmy is dating Attorney Emerson either. Right?" He raised his eyebrows and said, "First of all, I already know about that and it doesn't bother me and second of all, I don't see how that is any of your business and it shouldn't have been brought up in retaliation for what you did. I think we are changing that warning into a firing because I don't like your attitude either." She turned her anger into crying and he told her to go clean out her desk. He shook his head and left my office. He emailed me and asked me to come to his office and now I was scared that I was going to get fired.

I walked down and knocked on the door and he told me to come in. He told me to sit down and I did. He said, "Em, I am so pleased with all your work and you in general and you are such a big team player here, and you help everyone, whether it is your work or not. I have something for you and I wanted to ask you another favor." He handed me an envelope and told me not to open it until I was by myself. "I would like to make you the Paralegal Manager and that means you would be the head Paralegal and you would have 2 or 3 people under you. Of course, it is a brand new position and you would be making a lot more money. Your job would be to oversee that the paralegals are doing their work in a timely manner and that everything is getting done and if it isn't and they are overwhelmed with work, you would delegate that work to someone with less work. In other words, you would be their boss. What do you think about that?" I opened my mouth in shock and said, "I would love to take on that position, but of course, I would like to see what my job description is first and the pay." He smiled and said, "Yes of course. I have been talking to Attorney Smith about this since you covered for Attorney Emerson and we both feel that you are the one for the job." I said, "Thank you for this opportunity. I appreciate it very much. When you finish with the job description and pay scale, let me know and I will look it over." He smiled and said, "I look forward to you accepting this position."

I left his office with a big smile on my face. They really like me and they like my work. I got back to my desk and there was an email from Attorney Smith, telling me that he was so proud to have an employee, as dedicated as I was, in his office. He also told me that he was interviewing for two more paralegals, so I would have three people under me, if I took the position. I looked over my other emails and did a few quick things to catch up.

I got going on the two emails from a month ago and I made sure they were both done before I left the office that night. That really pissed me off, but at least I got it done and I couldn't get blamed for it being late. Right now, it was only me and Evelyn as paralegals, so we were going to get inundated with work.

I called her in my office and told her what happened to Olivia and she was shocked. She said, "She told me that she was pissed that you gave her extra work to do and I told her that you had no choice, because you were covering for a secretary, but she didn't care. She was so mad at you." I told her that I knew she was mad, but it didn't give her the right not to do the work and I told her that she didn't do two of the things that I gave her and she got fired for it. She couldn't believe that she never did the work. I told her, "Ev, You are my number one paralegal here and I might become your boss. What are your feelings about this?" She opened her mouth in shock and said, "For real? Oh Em, There is no one else I would love to have as a boss. Congratulations." I told her it was not set in stone yet, but I was thinking about it. Then I said, "Evelyn, because it's just you and me right now, we are going to get inundated with work. If need be, can you put in overtime?" She said, "No problem at all. I will do what I have to do to get things done." I thanked her for that. I wasn't going to get any grief from her and that was good. The new paralegals would come in knowing I was there boss right from the start.

I left the office that night, thinking about what it would be like to be a boss over 3 girls. Do I want that responsibility? I might if the pay was good. I would have to put up with drama and attitudes, but if the pay was really good, I would put up with it. I wonder what's in that envelope? A check? Hmm.. I should have opened it before I started driving. I will open it when I get home.

I walked in the door and I got a text from Billy. "It looks like you are pretty popular in this office." I frowned and texted back. "What are you talking about?" He texted back. "The managing attorney called a meeting of all attorneys before I left and they said they were making a new position called Paralegal Manager and they wanted to let us know that the job was offered to Emily West, who is the Top Team Player in the whole office. They praised you to the hilt." I couldn't believe what I just read. "Really? Wow. I am about to open an envelope that Attorney Kaufman handed me. I will see you when you get home."

I opened the envelope and almost fell on the floor. It was a check for $5,000 and it said it was because they appreciated that I dropped everything to help someone in need and that I delegated my work so it would get done. It was for being the Top Team Player in the office. Holy Fucking Shit. This can't be real, can it? This is awesome. I can't wait to tell my parents and Billy about this.

I called my mom and told her about the offer and right away she said, "Take it, just take it." I told her I wanted to see the job description and the pay before accepting the position because you don't know what they will slip in there. Mom said, "Oh honey, what can they put in there?" I said, "Oh, I don't know. Maybe 'you have to work a 60 hour week, or you have to be in charge of this or that and it has nothing to do with paralegal work.' I want to check out the job description first and see if the pay matches what I have to do." She said, "I guess your right. You know what you are doing and will make the right decision. I am so proud of you. Keep me posted on that." I told her I would and we hung up.

My buzzer was ringing and it was Billy. He came in like a whirlwind and was all excited. "Wow, Em, they were singing your praises all over the place at this meeting. They love you there. They couldn't stop talking about you." I spoke up and told them what a good job you did for me all month and that all my work was done every single day and it was perfect and timely." I smiled at him and said, "Aww. Thanks Billy. Look at this!" I showed him the check. He opened his mouth in shock and said, "Holy Fuck Em. Wow, I guess they really DO like you. This is awesome. I am so happy for you." I blushed. "I have to see the job description and pay before I accept the new position." He agreed with me and pulled me in for a little fuel. God he was such a great kisser. He said, "Do you wanna go get a bite to eat with me?" I said, "Sure, where we going?" He said, "Metro Diner. They have good food and I think you'll like it there. You ready or do you need a few minutes?" I said, "Let me freshen my makeup and use the bathroom and I will be right with you." A few minutes later, we left and he fueled the fire before we left and again, when we got into the car.

The diner was nice and the food was delicious. I got the Teriyaki Steak Bowl, which was seasoned sirloin steak drizzled with a sweet teriyaki glaze and served over white rice and veggie mix of shredded carrots, red cabbage, corn, green peppers and onions and topped with scallions. It was so good. Billy got the Steak Tips, which was seasoned and seared sirloin tips with mushrooms in rich brown gravy with mashed potatoes and steamed green beans. It looked yummy and he said it was really good.

We didn't get dessert but we got some coffee and we talked for a while about our day and the firings that happened in the office. He said, "They don't put up with any shit at all. No warnings, no nothing, you don't do your work and your fired." I told him that Olivia was put on a warning, but then she tried to get back at me by telling Attorney Kaufman that we were dating and he let her have it. He raised his eyebrows and said, "She knew?" I said, "Yes, I told her in confidence, because I thought she was my friend and she was saying that she wanted to be your secretary because you were cute." I laughed and said, "Yup, I claimed you first." He laughed and said, "See it pays to be honest. I am happy that you told Kaufman." I said, "Me too. It was my intention to anyway, so it wouldn't come back at me." We finished our coffee and left and as always, he stopped to fuel the fire on the way back to the car. He said, "I am falling for you Em, like really falling for you." I looked him in the eye and said, "I am falling for you too Billy." He hugged me tight and then we walked to the car.

6

BIG PROMOTION

The next day at work, I received an email from Attorney Smith and Attorney Kaufman and they invited me to meet them in Conference Room A at 10:00 a.m. It was our smallest Conference Room and they used it for small meetings and interviews. I accepted the invitation and started working on my emails. I knew the meeting was about the job description and the pay. I was making $65,000 now, so it would have to be pretty significant, if I was going to be a manager. I knew these attorneys were not cheap, especially after receiving the check for being the Top Team Player of the office.

The emails were piling in from all the attorneys because Evelyn and I were splitting the work and Olivia was gone. I did the most important emails first. Mainly the things that wouldn't take long and wouldn't take a lot of time to complete. There were tons of those and most of them were rescheduling meetings, depositions and motions for continuance of court proceedings. After I got about 20 of those done, I went in the kitchen to make a coffee and saw Evelyn in there making herself a coffee too. I said, "How is it going Ev? Are you able to keep up so far?" She smiled and said, "I can't wait till they hire another paralegal. It's friggin crazy, but so far, I am ok. It's a lot though." I patted her on the back and said, "Let me know if you are getting overwhelmed and I will take some stuff from you." She smiled at me and said, "Listen, I know we are gonna be crazy for a while and I should be alright, but if I feel like I'm going crazy, I will take you up on that offer." She laughed. I said, "I have a meeting at 10, so if there is something urgent that comes up, can you ask an attorney?" She smiled at me and said, "Good Luck Em." It was a few minutes to 10 and I took my coffee and headed to the Conference Room. I stopped into my office for a pad and pen and continued. Both attorneys were waiting for me and I walked in and took a seat and said, "Good Morning". They both smiled at me and said, "Good Morning Emily." Attorney Kaufman slid a package of papers across the table and said, "Here is the job description for Paralegal Manager and the last page is the mid-grade pay you would receive, should you choose to accept this mission." He laughed. I laughed with him and pulled the package of papers towards me. I kept my head high and acted in a professional manner as I scanned through them.

Job Description for Paralegal Manager:

*   Works well with others

*   Works well independently

*   Pays close attention to detail

*   Highly organized individual

*   Must multi-task

*   Excellent research and writing skills

*   Works well under Pressure

*   Maintains a professional attitude

*   Good communication skills

The candidate must be responsible for Case Management and workload of the paralegal team. The candidate must assign projects that include preparation of various legal documents, Court Proceedings and billing procedures. The candidate must track education hours and check for accuracy of work product. The candidate must keep the paralegals 'in-line' and make sure all work is completed.

Ok, that sounded really good. Actually it was what I expected and nothing was added in there that I didn't like.

Last Page:

This job has been offered to Emily West, Paralegal for Attorney Emerson, Attorney Kaufman, Attorney Smith, Attorney Ganey, Attorney James and Attorney Segum. Emily currently makes $65,668,00, and if she accepts this position, she will be making $125,896.00.

______________________________EMILY WEST

______________________________ATTORNEY JOSEPH KAUFMAN

NAMED PARTNER FOR SMITH & KAUFMAN LAW FIRM, LLC

______________________________ATTORNEY ANDREW SMITH

MANAGING ATTORNEY FOR SMITH & KAUFMAN LAW FIRM, LLC

______________________________WITNESS

______________________________NOTARY PUBLIC

I read the whole thing over twice and then looked up at them and nodded my head as I said, "I choose to accept this mission, gentlemen, so get your pens ready." They both chuckled and smiled at me. Attorney Kaufman went to call Evelyn into the office, to notarize the document and one of the secretaries to witness, while Attorney Smith covered the top part of the last page, so no one would know how much I was making and he taped a piece of paper over the top. We all signed, then the secretary witnessed it and then I took the oath for the Notary and she signed and sealed the documents. Evelyn smiled at me and whispered, "*Congrats*" and she walked out and the attorney's both said, "Thank you Ladies." When they left and closed the door, I said,"Thank you both for making this worth my while. I happily accept this position and you won't be sorry for picking me. I won't let you down. I promise." They both smiled at me and Attorney Kaufman said, "We know we picked the right person and we know you won't let us down. We are proud to have you with us."

He paused and said, "Ya know, yesterday, when I saw you in Evelyn's office, I peeked in to see what was going on because I thought she was giving you a hard time like Olivia, but then I realized, she was onboard with you and she likes you and then I realized what a Team Player you were, by going in there to get work away from her, so she wasn't overwhelmed and further more, I was super impressed when you called her into your office to let her know that you might be her boss and wanted her thoughts on that." I smiled at him and just said, "Well, I have been working with her since I started here and I didn't want any hard feelings, so I figured I would put it out there and I felt better about accepting this position, knowing that she was backing me." He looked at Attorney Smith and pointed at me. "See, that is what I mean about her. Perfect fit." He looked at me and said, "Don't think that these things you do, go unnoticed." He pointed to the door and said, "I think we are finished here, unless you have any questions about your new job, which by the way, starts now, December 1st. Get to work" and then he laughed.

I got up and shook both their hands and left. I got back to my office and there was a new sign on my door. Instead of saying, "Paralegal" in gold lettering, it said, "EMILY WEST, MANAGING PARALEGAL". It was an actual sign that they had made for me. I guess they knew I wouldn't be able to refuse such a good offer. They were right, because I was making double what I was before and doing what I love with people that I liked.

There were a lot of interviews going on for new paralegals that day in Conference Room A. Evelyn said she counted 20 girls that went in and out of the conference room that day. The partners knew we needed help as soon as possible. Our office was growing because they hired another attorney after Billy, and they were adding a new secretary too.

Billy came by my office and snapped a picture of my door and he texted it to me. "Congratulations sweetheart. I am so fucking proud of you. You won their hearts, along with mine. " I replied, "Thanks Babe." but then I erased it because we were at the office. "Thank you very much. See you at lunch.

Keeping this professional." We met in the cafeteria for lunch and he asked me how it was going. I told him it was just Evelyn right now and she was easy going. I checked on her a few times and looked over her work and it was fine. He told me we were celebrating at dinner tonight and I told him we didn't have to do that, but he insisted.

Billy took me to Flemings Prime Steakhouse and Wine Bar. This place was exquisite and very expensive. I told Billy that this was not necessary and he argued with me that it WAS necessary. "It's not every day that your girlfriend gets a promotion. This is big Em. Really big and I am so proud of you." I was blushing and said, "Thanks Billy. I am proud of me too." I laughed. The waiter came to the table and Billy ordered the Sweet Chili Calamari for starters and a bottle of Cabernet Sauvignon.

The waiter came back with the bottle and our calamari and another waiter came to the table with a candle, a teddy bear and a bouquet of roses in a vase and lit the candle and handed me the Teddy Bear. I looked at him puzzled, and he smiled at me and said, "Congratulations. I can't tell you how proud I am of you, so I will show you." I got tears in my eyes and a few leaked out. He caught them with a napkin from across the table and he said, "I love you Em." He got up and put a match to the fire brewing under my skin. "I am so overwhelmed by this Billy. I love you too." I hugged the Teddy Bear and told him I loved it. I couldn't believe all this. He was so awesome and I loved the whole show he put on for me.

He poured the wine and we ate Calamari and then we put our dinner order in. We both ordered a Filet Mignon with a side of North Atlantic Lobster Mashed Potatoes and Crispy Brussel Sprouts and Bacon. When I tell you this was delicious, it is an understatement. This place was exquisite and the ambiance was to die for. We both got the Chocolate Lava Cake for dessert. It was all Devine, yes Devine. The best I ever had.

We went back to Billy's place and we watched a movie on Netflix, well, we intended to anyway, but it never happened because the fire got too hot and we ended up in bed and had some very hot steamy sex. I thought his kisses were hot, but those kisses were just an appetizer of how hot this man was. He brought me there many, many times and I wasn't quiet about it. He got loud a few times too. He kept fueling the fire, so it wouldn't go out. He kissed and licked and rubbed and I couldn't get enough of it. It went on and on and on until we were exhausted. Just so you know… the fire never went out… It was still fizzling…and he was still holding me… and still kissing me….

It was midnight when he walked me back to my apartment. I made him stay with me and he went home in the morning to get ready for work. I showered, got dressed, made breakfast and made my lunch and I was out the door. I got to the office before Billy and put my lunch in the fridge and went to my office. When I got there, my desk was piled high with files that needed work done. I looked them over, and then peeked in at Evelyn and she had a pile too. Ok, so, I will just take care of them myself. I had a slew of emails and looked quickly through them. This was way more work than I ever had, but I knew it was coming. I wondered too, if this was a test I needed to pass, but I didn't worry about it.

My main priority was to get all this done and show them I could do it. 'Working under pressure'.   First, I went through and did all the quick emails. Then I prioritized the rest of them and did the same things with the files on my desk. Quick in one pile and the others in another pile. I confirmed all the appointments

for tomorrow for all six attorneys first. I typed up all the shorter motions next, proof-read them and e-filed them with the court, I started on the mail and added all the appointments to all their calendars and called to change a few dates that were not available. I called a few clients and made appointments to meet with them to go over Disclosure and Production. I had about 12 of these to do and I spread the appointments over the rest of the week. And now…it was lunchtime. Wow, that was fast. The morning flew by. I ate my lunch at my desk and I noticed that Evelyn did too. I stepped in to say hi and ask her how she was doing. She laughed and said, "Overwhelmed, How are you?" I laughed with her and said, "Hopefully they hire soon. Let me know if you need help with anything Ev. I mean it." She smiled at me and said, "Don't worry about me. I will be fine."

7

CHRISTMAS AND NEW YEARS

I went back to my office and my phone was ringing. It was my mom and I told her I accepted the job. She wanted me to come home for Christmas and she sounded sobby. I asked if she was crying and she said she wasn't, but she said she missed me. I told her I had some vacation time and I would let her know and told her I was still with Billy. She said, "Oh, so you will probably go to his parents for Christmas?" I said, "Mom, I don't know yet. I haven't been invited as of yet, but don't worry. Even if I am not there for Christmas Day, I will still see you. Ok?" She said OK, but I knew she wouldn't be happy unless it was for Christmas.

Later that night, I discussed the Holidays with Billy and asked what he was doing because my mom hadn't seen me and she was sad. He said, "I can go with you to Connecticut for Christmas, as long as we are back for New Year's Eve. How's that?" I said, "What's New Year's Eve?" He said, "Well, my parents do a

Christmas dinner, but they also do New Year's Eve and Day and they have a big bash and all of us sleepover and party all night. My eyes lit up and I said, "Oh wow. Ok, so we are going?" He shook his head. "We can both take 2 weeks off and you should put in for it right away." I said, "Yeah, I don't have anyone to cover for me now." He said, "Yes you do. You have Evelyn. She is your number one paralegal and besides, things slow way down around the holidays." I said, "Yes, you are right. I will ask her tomorrow and tell Charlene that I will be taking 2 weeks at Christmas."

The next day, I went in to see Evelyn and she was typing away and stopped when she saw me and smiled. I said, "Mornin Ev. Are you ok?" She smiled and said, "Yup, as good as can be. I have been coming in an hour early everyday, so it's working." I was surprised and thanked her for doing that. "You are a Team Player Ev and I will make it known.

I wanted to ask you a favor. I am taking two weeks off around Christmas and I am going back to Connecticut to see my family. Would you consider covering for me as Paralegal

Manager?" She laughed and said, "Sure, I don't mind being my own boss. I am taking time after the New Year and only one or two days before Christmas." I laughed and thanked her and told her I was requesting the time from Charlene.

I sent the email off to Charlene and let her know the days I wanted and told her that Evelyn would cover for me. She approved my days. Billy got his days approved and that night we made reservations to fly north for the holidays. We were going for a week and then flying back to spend New Year's Eve and Day with his parents and the rest of the time was ours.

Billy and I worked for another week and he cooked me suppers almost every night. I packed my backpack with clothes for a week and carried my winter coat on the plane. I packed my suitcase with the gifts I got for my family and we were off. Billy just had his back pack and carried his winter coat too. We had a nice flight to Connecticut and there was a light snow falling when we got there.

My brothers, Jesse and Jack picked us up in Jesse's SUV and I introduced them to Billy. They all shook hands and they kissed me and told me how much they missed me and we headed for the truck. We had an hour ride back to my mom and dad's house. Jesse and Jack were talking to Billy the whole way and just getting acquainted. What did he like, what didn't he like. They asked him what was he interested in. I loved his answer to that. He said, "Your sister." They laughed at him and Jesse said, "Good answer Dude." They talked about music and hobbies and movies and his job. They congratulated me on my promotion and asked me how much I was making now. I told them I was making $125,000 and Billy almost choked. He said, "WHAT? I never asked you, but I never thought it was that much. WOW." I laughed and said, "I never asked you either." He whispered in my ear, "*$155,000.*" Jesse said, "What was that? I didn't hear." He laughed and then Billy told him. Jesse said, "You impress me Billy."

My Mom and Dad were standing in the doorway waiting. We had about an inch of snow by the time we got there, so Billy was holding onto me as we walked up the sidewalk. Jesse and Jack were watching as I struggled and kept slipping and Billy was holding me up. Dad opened the door and I barely got through the door and my mom pulled me in and was hugging me so tight. "I missed you so much baby." I introduced Billy and he shook hands with my Dad and hugged my mom and kissed her on the cheek. He was so cheerful and said, "Merry Christmas everyone." He wasn't nervous at all and he fit right in with everyone. Jesse's wife Maria and Jack's wife, Isabella (Izzy) came in to meet Billy and they were giving him the 'eye'. They both gave me a thumbs up and told me later how cute he was and how nice he was.

Jesse took our backpacks and my suitcase and Jack helped him take everything upstairs to our bedroom. They came down and they made margaritas for all the women and they did a few shots with Billy and my dad. My mom had a bunch of appetizers and picky foods out and that got Billy's attention. He walked up to the table and said, "Ahhh what do we have here? Deviled Eggs, a Charcuterie Board, yum, bacon wrapped scallops, tiny egg rolls, Shrimp Cocktail and piggy's in a blanket. Who made all this?" Maria said, "We all brought some stuff, so it's not all on mom." He looked at everyone and said, "Thank you for all this. It's so nice and it all looks fantastic." My mom told him to grab a plate and he needed no coaxing to do that. My mom said because it was 2:00, she didn't want to serve lunch, so she would just have this. I said, "I love it mom. It's perfect." She said, "We were all gonna go out for dinner, but then it started snowing, so Dad ordered food and had it delivered already. We will just heat it up in the oven later." Billy came up to me and said, "Open up". And like a little bird, I did, and he shoved a bacon wrapped scallop in my mouth. He said, "Yummm". I laughed and looked at my mom and dad and said, "He is a Foodie." He laughed and agreed with me.

We all had a nice afternoon sitting around in the living room and my Dad and brothers kept the fireplace going. I put pillows on the floor in front of it for me and Billy and patted one for Billy to sit next to me, but my comedian brother, Jesse, ran over and sat on it and started laughing hysterically, while he put his arm around me and pulled me in for a hug. I think he missed me too. Billy just stood there laughing and tapped him on the shoulder and said, "Can I cut in?" Jesse got up and said, "Absolutely Dude." Jesse always called everyone Dude. That was his trademark. Jesse was the middle child and Jack was the oldest and more serious and I, of course, was the baby. Jesse and I were a year apart and we were very close. I am the one who introduced him to Maria. I worked with her at my first little shit job at the drugstore, down the street, as a cashier. They fell madly in love and got married within a year and they have been married for 2 years now.

Jack met Izzy in college and they got married when they graduated 5 years ago. Jack doesn't want kids, but I never asked Izzy if she wanted them. I am assuming the answer is no, because they had to have discussed such an important thing. Jesse said they want kids, but they want to go on a few more vacations overseas, before they settle down. They want to enjoy freedom for a while. I can't blame them there. I want kids, I think, but not right away. If I ever get married, I would like to enjoy my marriage for at least 5 years before having them. Especially now that I got my promotion and I am making a lot of money and I loved my job. Jesse and I were discussing all this and Billy was listening in. He said, "What do you mean, if you ever get married?" I looked at him and said, "Yes, if I ever get married." He looked sad and said, "Am I a prospective partner?" I smiled at him and said, "We haven't discussed any of this and we have only been going out a few months. We still have plenty of time." He shook his head and I think I made him feel bad. I went over to him and whispered. *"This does not mean I don't love you or even thought about marrying you, because I have."* He smiled at me and then bent down and kissed me and started another fire in the living room. I think if this man asked me to marry him right now, I would say yes. There is no one else I would rather be with for the rest of my life. I know I have only known him for a short time, but my heart says, "Yes".

My mom and dad put all the food trays in the oven to warm up dinner and me and my sister-in-laws set the table. The guys stayed in the living room playing X-Box games and there was a lot of yelling and swearing. We just looked at each other and rolled our eyes and then started laughing. Mom pulled me aside and said, "I like this guy you met. He is the one for you, I just know it. He fits right in like he's been here forever and Dad likes him too." I whispered to her. "*I love him mom*." She started clapping her hands and doing a little hop, like a little girl that got candy. I laughed at her and then hugged her. My mom was 52 years old and my dad was 55. Jack was 29, Jesse was 24 and I was 23. I always ask her if I was an accident and she would always say that I was her blessing. I think I was an accident, because me and Jesse were only a year apart, which means she got pregnant with me when Jesse was 3 months old. When I say that to her she repeats, "You were and are my blessing and I would do it all over again." My Dad always says the same thing and calls me <u>his</u> blessing.

We had a nice dinner and our spare chair around the dining room table was filled by Billy and my mom was brimming with pride, as she looked around at all the filled chairs. She had 2 sons, 2 daughter-in-laws, 1 blessing, and a prospective son-in-law for her blessing.

We got snowed in that night and pretty much just stayed in the house for the few days before Christmas, but we all decorated the Christmas Tree and I put my gifts around it. We put up lights down the staircase and decorated the whole inside of the house with the Manger and bells and a Santa sleigh for Christmas cards. Jesse and Billy decorated the front porch with the blow up Santa and Reindeers and put lights all around the door. We were all feeling very festive and me and the girls and mom were baking cookies and making apple pie and cheesecake for desserts. My mom made a ham, Shrimp Scampi and a lasagna for Christmas Eve and Christmas Day and we had salad and garlic bread and sweet potatoes and mashed potatoes and we threw in the kitchen sink because there wasn't enough food. LOL. Just Kidding... We could have fed the whole neighborhood. Billy was in his glory and kept telling my mom what a good cook she was and he was hanging around in the kitchen while we cooked and baked because that is what he loved. He even helped my mom slice the mozzarella for the lasagna and grate cheese and rolled meatballs.

We opened gifts on Christmas Eve and I gave Billy a 3-D Crystal Scales of Justice for his desk and had it personalized with his name. I got him a personalized leather portfolio. I got him a personalized Leather charging station valet, a hooded sweatshirt, a personalized aluminum Pen Set with the Scales of Justice on them. I got him a leather wrist band and I got him a handcrafted custom Cutting Board with his name engraved into it. My parents gave me gifts cards and money and my brothers did the same. Billy didn't give me anything and said, "I have something for you when we get home. I forgot to bring it." I just smiled at him and said, "You don't need to get me anything." He just smiled.

On Christmas morning, we were all sitting in the living room sipping coffee and Billy said, "Shit, I will be right back." He went upstairs and came back and sat next to me and handed me a box. It was a medium sized box and everyone was all excited. I opened it and it was an 8 x 10 picture of us that he took with the roses behind us at the Raleigh Rose Garden. It was such a nice picture and I loved it. I kissed him and thanked him. Then he got down on one knee and proposed to me. He said, "I know we have only been dating for a couple of months, but I love you with all my heart and soul and I know you are the one for me and I have never ever felt this way with anyone, my whole life. Will you do me the honor of being my friend, my wife and my lover, forever and ever?" My eyes filled with tears and I said, "OMG, Billy, I never expected this in a million years, but YES, YES, I feel the same way about you and I will marry you."

He put the most beautiful ring on my finger and I hugged him so tight and everyone started cheering. My mom was crying. My dad had tears in his eyes and Jesse was getting up to get the bottle of Jack with shot glasses and it was only 10 a.m. Billy said, "You made me nervous yesterday when you were saying, "If I ever get married, so I decided to wait till today to give this to you. It was supposed to be last night." I said, "I would have said YES, last night too." He said, "I promise to make you happy, to protect you, to love you and I promise to find your car if you ever lose it again." Everyone busted out laughing. My mom was still crying. "My baby is getting married. OMG"

Mom made French toast for breakfast and we all sat in the dining room passing the syrup, the butter and confectionery sugar and pouring more coffee.

We had a great day all together and my mom brought out baby pictures of all of us, but mostly of me so Billy could see what I looked like. He said, "Jeez, you were such a cute little baby. And you still are." We were all in the living room with the fireplace going. Jack was watching a game on TV and Jesse was all into the baby pictures with us. We took out the leftover appetizers and chowed down on those and we had the lasagna for dinner and my mom warmed up the ham for anyone who wanted it. We also had Shrimp Scampi that she served on Christmas Eve. She always went all out for Christmas Eve and Day. These were the Holidays that she loved the most and she needed her family around her. She was so happy that we came and she kept thanking Billy for bringing me home.

We left 2 days after Christmas and my mom was happy. Jesse and Jack took us back to the airport and we were on our way.

We made sure we called her when we got home and she appreciated that. She loved Billy and I was happy about that. My whole family loved him and he couldn't say enough about them. We were made for each other and it showed.

Our next visit was to Billy's family and we packed an overnight bag so we could spend New Year's Eve and Day with them. I thought it was just family, but they had friends and neighbors and other family members there. Just the immediate family slept over and everyone else went home, but it was a big crowd and there were a lot of drunk people staggering around.

Billy announced our engagement when we got there and everyone was stunned. I am not sure if they were happy about it or not, even if they said they were. I think they were really shocked that he proposed so soon. Hell, so was I, but my heart said YES.   He was fueling the fire every chance he got and he was such a romantic. When he told everyone, his father said, "Really? Wow. Ok." That is what made me think they weren't really happy about it. I saw his father pull him aside and talk to him, but I don't know what they talked about. I will ask him later, but I have a feeling it was about our engagement. They say there is always one in the crowd and this time I think there were 2 or more in the crowd. I don't think his parents or sisters were happy about it. I began to wonder if they thought it was just too soon or maybe they didn't like me.

We had a good time New Year's Eve and I made sure I helped and was part of everything that was happening. New Year's Day was just immediate family, and everyone was cooking and baking and gabbing and the TV was blaring with a game on. His Dad was big on football and he was yelling. Billy was in with his Dad and his brother-in-laws and watching with him and all us girls were in the kitchen. I saw his mom looking at me and I said, "Is there something wrong?" She said, "Do you love Billy, I mean really love him?" What the Fuck kind of snarky remark is that? Are you kidding me right now? I said, "I love him with all my heart and soul. Yes, of course I love him." She nodded her head and then said, "Do you know this is a big commitment and do you know what you are in for?" I tilted my head and said, "I love your son and will always love your son for the rest of my life. I have no intention of hurting him, ever." What the hell was happening here? His two sisters were standing right there, but they kept their heads down and stayed out of the conversation. His mother was going to be a pain in my ass, I could tell right away. Who the fuck asks those kind of questions?

Oh yea, your mom is cool alright. NOT!! I think if he knew she was asking me this shit, he would say something. I looked at her and said, "Do you have a problem with me? Do you not like me? Did I do something to you?" I wanted her to know that I was not going to stand for this shit and I was going to stand my ground.   She looked shocked and said, "Oh no no, I like you and no you didn't do anything. I am sorry if I made you feel like that. I just worry about him. He wears his heart on his sleeve and he has gotten hurt before and it hit him hard. I just don't want to see him hurt again." I said, "I have no intentions of hurting him." I walked out of the room and sat with Billy on the couch and I was fucking pissed. "We should probably get going early so we don't hit any traffic." He looked at me shocked and said, "We didn't eat yet babe. Is there something going on that I should know about?" I just shook my head no, because I didn't want to start anything. I saw his dad turn away from the game and he looked at me and he knew something was going on. He got up and went in the kitchen and I heard something slam and I think it was him hitting the countertop and his mother left the kitchen and went to the bathroom.

Billy took my face in his hands and said, "What the fuck just happened? Come with me upstairs." He took my hand and we walked up to the bedroom. I told him what happened and he was so fucking pissed. There was a knock on the bedroom door and it was his dad. Billy told him to come in and his dad wanted to know what happened so Billy told him. I started crying because I felt like I started something. Billy said, "My mom can be a little overbearing sometimes."

His Dad interrupted and said, "Don't cry sweetheart. We all love you and she is just overprotective of her boy, but she knows she overstepped. You did nothing wrong." I told him I wanted to go home. "I can't sit at the table with all of you knowing what she said to me." His Dad said, "You have nothing to be ashamed of. It is all my wife's fault and she will apologize for this."

I told him I didn't want to start any fights with the family and he said I didn't start it, his wife did. His father took my hand and led me downstairs with Billy in tow. His mom was at the bottom of the stairs and she had been crying and she said that she was sorry and that she was just worried about her son. I told her to stop worrying about him. He is a grown man and he knows what he wants. She walked away. Billy's sisters and their husbands were all standing around listening to what was going on.

His sister Liz tugged at my arm and brought me into a room next to the bathroom. She was whispering to me. *"Our husbands went through the same thing she is putting you through. She can be a pain in the ass sometimes, but just ignore her. My husband told her off and it took quite a while before they were talking."* I whispered back, *"I refuse to put up with that shit. I will tell her off too. She is not going to talk to me like that and think she can get away with it and the sooner she realizes that, the better it will be."* Liz was nice and so was his sister Sarah. She said, *"My brother adores you and I have never seen him so happy. You guys do whatever you want and don't worry about what family thinks."* I laughed and said, *"She doesn't know me, but she will. We WILL do whatever we want and I will never let family interfere. Not even my own and by the way, my family loves Billy and they were happy for us."* Liz whispered. *"We are happy for you too, but my mom was in shock because it's only been a couple of months. I knew this was coming, but I couldn't do anything about it."* I knew she was trying to make me feel better so I just said, "Thanks Liz, I appreciate what you are trying to do."

We left the room and I walked into the kitchen where his mom was. She glanced at me and then looked away. I went right up to her and said, "I have no intention of hurting your son. I love him with everything I have in my body and I always will. I am sorry that you don't like that we got engaged so soon, but <u>really</u>, it's none of your business. This is HIS life and MY life and we will live it as we see fit. If you want to have a relationship with us, then you will just have to accept that and if you don't want to accept it, it will be your loss." She turned to me, put her hand on my shoulder and said,

"I'm sorry, I really am." I put my hand on her shoulder and said, "Forgiven". I walked into the dining room and helped his sisters set the table for dinner and no one said a word, not even Liz. But I knew they heard what I said to their mother, because I was not whispering and the sound on the TV, in the living room was reduced so they could hear it in there too. Fuck this bullshit and that is what it was. After I said my peace, she knew I wasn't taking any of her shit anymore. I think everyone knew I wasn't taking anyone's shit after that speech. I was proud of myself. I didn't act shy or cower in a corner, I let her have it and she needed it.

Billy had made it sound like his mother was an angel, but she wasn't and my mom was looking more like the angel now. She accepted him as family immediately and she minded her own business. I mean everyone has their flaws. My mom was not perfect either, and in my book, no one is perfect. I told Billy that this would be the last sleepover affair at his mother's house. I told him he could do New Year's Eve and Day if he wanted to, and I would too, but I was going home after each event. He agreed that it was too much to stay over because his mother was a pain in the ass. He told me that she tried to pull this shit with his last girlfriend.

"I wasn't even engaged to the other girlfriend, but she still tried to intimidate her and I am not sure why. What is wrong with her? I don't understand why she is acting like this. Even my Dad got pissed off at her and punched the kitchen counter. It's just uncalled for. Hopefully after your awesome speech, she will stop this shit." He laughed and said, "Yeah, I heard it. My dad turned the TV down and we all heard it."

After dinner, we cleaned up and she wanted everyone to stay overnight again and I looked at Billy and shook my head no. He didn't want to stay anyway. We had 2 days left of vacation and we wanted to spend it alone.

8

WANNA BUY A HOUSE?

We packed up and left after dessert. It was only a 15 minute drive to get home and I was happy to be away from his mother. His dad

was awesome and his sister's and their husbands were nice as could be, but even though she apologized, I did not like his mother and he knew it. He didn't say a word and I guess he figured he would let things cool down. We both showered and had some fiery sex in there and then got comfy in bed and watched TV.

We spent the night at his apartment and we talked about me moving in with him and getting rid of my apartment. I had 3 months left on my lease and we talked about paying it off. He wanted to pay for it and I told him I would and then we agreed that we would go half and pay $1,500 each. He said I could use the other bedroom as my office, so we would both have an office. He had a twin bed in the spare room and I told him we should leave it there in case we had a guest. He laughed and said, "Yeah, just in case my mom wants to visit." I didn't laugh and he knew it was too soon to joke about that.

There was no more talk about his mother for weeks. She called him a few times and he was short with her. She apologized to him every single time she called and he was still short with her. She knew she fucked up, but we all knew it would blow over.

We both went back to work after the Holidays and I got an email notice that they hired one new attorney, one new secretary and 2 paralegals. Attorney Kaufman took me around to meet the new employees and I introduced myself. Attorney Pam Sanders and her secretary, Linda Bartone and also, my two new paralegals, Mia Santana and Ginny Stevens and of course my number one paralegal, Evelyn Lopez. This was their first day on the job, so it was my responsibility to show them the ropes. We had a computer class that morning and into the early afternoon until they understood how to use the program. Then I assigned them 3 attorneys each and unassigned those attorneys from me and Evelyn.

Now we each at 3 attorneys and the work would be more even. I had 6 and Ev had 5 when I left. But then they hired another attorney when I was out. I sent emails to the attorneys and told them who their new paralegal would be and they came around to meet them. Everything was falling into place. The ladies were very nice and I told them if they ever had any questions, they could come to me and if I wasn't here they could ask Evelyn or an attorney. I also told them if they felt overwhelmed or they weren't able to get their work done in a timely manner that they had to report to me. Our firm was getting bigger by the minute.

We announced our engagement to Attorney Kaufman and Attorney Smith in Conference Room A, and they both congratulated us. We told them we didn't pick a date yet, but it would be in about a year.

We didn't go and visit his parents for a few months and then Easter came and we got an invite. He asked me if I wanted to go before he made any decisions by himself and I told him I would go. I brought a dessert and he got her a cactus plant. She kissed me on the cheek as we came through the door and asked us how things were going and Billy told her that we were living together and that we paid off my lease. She said, "Oh, that's nice. Good for you." She was on her best behavior and I think his Dad had a lot to do with that. He probably told her that if she started any shit that we would leave and she would never see her son again. I bet he threatened her like that and I hope he did. She was super nice all day. There were no snarky remarks or looks and it was nice for a change. His Dad kept smiling at me and he gave me a thumbs up a couple of times, so now I knew it was him. LOL.

When we left, she handed Billy an envelope and he opened it in the car. She gave us an Amazon Gift Card for Easter. It was for $200.00. He said, "Yeah, she usually gives me a $100, so the other $100 is yours." I corrected him and said, "It's ours." He shook his head yes.

He kissed me and started a fire in the car before we got home. "I love you Em and I didn't want any of this to happen. I'm so sorry." I looked at him and said, "This was not your fault, none of it, so stop worrying about it because your father fixed it." He laughed and said, "I know, but it never should have happened in the first place." I told him to stop and that he was not to blame. "I love you too, Billy and I always will." He drove home and then added some more fuel to the fire before we got out of the car. God he was hot!

As we were on our way home, he said, "Next Holiday we go visit your parents. At least they like me." He laughed a little, but I knew he was hurt by what his mother did. I said, "My whole family loves you Billy." He said, "What is the next Holiday?" I said, "I think it is Memorial Day and then the Fourth of July." He said, "Lets plan on flying to Connecticut for the Fourth of July. It will be nice and hot there at that time." I got excited and said, "OK, I will call my mom and tell her and we will all plan a party." He said, "I think for Memorial Day, we will go on a vacation. Just you and me and the sky's the limit, so where do you want to go? Any ideas?" I said, "I haven't really thought about it, and I really never went anywhere, but I have always wanted to go to California. What do you think?" He smiled and said, "California it is. I have never been there either." He paused and he was still thinking about his mother. "Ya know, I have always agreed with my mom about everything, even though I really didn't. Ya know what I mean? Like to just please her, I would yes her to death. Do you think this has something to do with this shit? I just can't believe her and I am still pissed about it. Doesn't she want me to be happy?" I shrugged my shoulders and said, "I don't know babe. I think she wants you to be happy, but maybe she thought you would never get married because your sister's got married first? I don't know. I guess we will never know. There are certain things that people do and no one understands them." I paused and then said, "The first rule of marriage is that you live your life the way you want to, not the way your parents want you to. I will never do anything my parents tell me to do and that is not a defiant thing by any means. It just means I have to find out for myself, and I want to live my life the way I want to. I will take advice, into consideration, but not orders. Does that make sense?" He laughed and said, "It most certainly does make sense."

We got home and he pulled our backpacks out of the trunk and carried both of them up to our apartment. We both took a shower and….Yep.

We got comfy in our sweats and just laid in bed and watched TV. He looked at me and said, "Em, my lease is almost up. What do you think about buying a house together? Do you think that is something you want to do?" I smiled at him and said, "A house? Do you think we should so soon? They are a lot of work to take care of. I don't know. I would have to think on that for a bit." He looked disappointed and said, "Ok."

He continued to watch TV and I looked at him a couple of times and I think I really disappointed him. I said, "Where would we look for this house?" He smiled at me and said, "In Raleigh, if you want, or we could move far away from my mother." He laughed. I laughed with him and said, "Ok, let's look and see if we find something we both like and we have to get pre-approved by a bank." He leaned over and kissed me with those hot lips and he hugged me. Now he was happy and it was showing. He said, "Holly Springs is a nice town and we would be about a half hour away from Raleigh, or we could look in Hillsborough and that is about 45 minutes or even Carrboro which is 40 minutes away, and it has a Farmer's Market and plenty of places to go hiking and have picnics. Carrboro has a lot of young professionals in their town. That would be us." And he pointed to me. I said, "We can look at all those places, but I think I would like Carrboro because of the Farmer's Market." He laughed and said, "I love that stuff too. We can look there first." I asked him if he liked to go hiking and on picnics and he said, "Absolutely, do you like that too?" I shook my head yes. "I love hiking as long as it's not too steep." He leaned over and kissed me and said, "Let's do it then."

We got up the next morning and he said, "Do you want to go to the bank and get pre-approved for our mortgage or wait? I don't want to push you, but I do." He started laughing and then stopped and said, "My lease is up in 2 months so I figured if we were gonna do this, we should start at least looking." I smiled at him and I knew he was so excited about this. I was too, I can't lie.

I was looking forward to becoming a homeowner. It is a big step in life. I said, "I'm Ready, let's do this." He had the biggest smile on his face. He took me out for breakfast to a place called Grata Diner in Carrboro. I looked at him and said, "Billy, we forgot about one very important thing." He turned around and said, "What did we forget?" I said, "Our jobs. This means we would be traveling 40 minutes each way to work and back." He smiled and said, "Yeah but we would only take one car. I don't mind if you don't." I teetered my head back and forth and said, "I guess. If you don't mind, then I don't."

We got seated at the diner and so far, I liked the town and the restaurant. I got blueberry pancakes, sausages and bacon. Billy got the western omelet with toast and bacon. It was very good.

We were both looking on-line for houses to see and I found one that was $650,00 and it had 5 bedrooms, 4 baths and was 2383 sq. st. with hardwood floors and new carpet. We looked at the pictures together and we both liked it. We both liked the style of the house and the fact that it had so many bedrooms. The large deck overlooked a flat backyard. It was complete with all appliances and had a breakfast nook and over a half acre of land. It was freshly painted and had new LED lighting. It had a family room with a gas fireplace. This place was in Chapel Hill and that was 28 miles from Raleigh, which is the same as Carrboro and would take about 40 minutes. We really wanted to see this house. We finished up breakfast and headed to a bank in town and walked in to get some information on how to get pre-approved.

Neither of us had done this before, so we had no idea about how to go about it. We found out that what we needed was a pre-qualification first, which is just a general confirmation that you meet basic requirements to receive a loan. The next thing would be a pre-approval which is when the lender will pull your credit to see whether you are creditworthy enough to receive a loan, but it doesn't guarantee that you will get a loan. We were brought into the office by the loan officer and he explained everything to us. He took all Billy's information and mine and told us that we shouldn't have a problem because we both made good money, we didn't have any debt and our credit was excellent. So we got both things done and it took a while to do it. We were in his office for a couple of hours. The First and Second Step were done.

He told us that a lot of sellers and agents will not even sit down to negotiate with someone unless they think you are serious and the pre-approval letter signals to everyone that you are seriously interested, that you have already been touch with a lender and that you most likely have the finances to receive a mortgage loan.

We sat in the car and Billy called the Realtor for the house in Chapel Hill that we fell in love with and asked if it was possible to see the house either today or tomorrow before we went back to work and said we were on vacation. It was 12:30 and she asked if we could meet her at 2:00 and he made the appointment and he was smiling at me and shaking his head yes and I was getting excited. He got off the phone with her and said, "Her name is Jessica and she said she would meet us there at 2:00 p.m. Let's take a ride to see the neighborhood and drive around to see what restaurants are around and other stuff. Ok?" I said, "Yes, we should see the neighborhood. It said it was a nice quiet neighborhood and I want to see if it is well kept.

He put the address in the GPS and we found the house. Jessica was there and she was showing the house to someone else. My heart sank and all of a sudden, I wanted to cry. Billy said, "That may not be her. It may be another real estate agent because she didn't mention that she was showing the house. She said it would take her about 30 minutes to get there. Let's just keep our fingers crossed." I crossed my fingers and prayed that we would get the house if we really wanted it. We drove around the neighborhood and it was so, so nice. It was neat and clean and people were taking a walk on the sidewalks that adorned the front of each house on the road. It was beautiful and I absolutely loved the white picket fences. It was my kind of town and it was country like. The house we were going to look at did not have a picket fence, but it was my favorite color of baby blue. It didn't have a garage, but Billy said we could always add one or get a carport. There were 4 stairs that went up to the front door and the stairs and walkway were brick in a pretty design. The windows were bay windows and I couldn't wait to see the inside of them.

For someone who had to think about buying, I was more excited about it than Billy. There was another house we wanted to look at too and it had 5 bedrooms, 3 baths and 2212 sq ft. I found it while we were driving around and it was much more elegant that the first one and it was empty and $5,000 cheaper. Now I really wanted the second one. Billy stopped in a parking lot to look at the pictures and he even said the second one was awesome. He called that agent and we got an appointment for 3:00 p.m. We kept our appointment for the first one and went to see it. It's not what we expected, but it was really nice. It was very old fashioned inside and we were looking for something more up to date.

We went to see the second house and we fell in love with it. It was everything we were looking for. It was up to date and super nice. Billy asked if there were any offers on the house yet and they said no offers yet. The agents name was Theo and he said, the owners were really motivated because they already moved out and needed to sell it. He told us it was on the market for 6 months and the only offer that came in was way too low for the sellers. We put in an offer for $600,000 and they bit. They wanted 610,000 and we countered at 605,000. Holy Shit…We just bought a fucking house.

Well, we still had to get the loan, but I didn't foresee any problems. We did all the usual stuff and got the appraisal and the inspection and they found nothing wrong with it. We even had an outdoor shed and a brick patio that was ground level and a fire pit and a gas heater that they left. It had a laundry room with the washer and dryer. It had a playground, an in-ground pool, a hot tub and the living room furniture was staying, along with a beautiful glass coffee table and white lamps. It had a beautiful dining room, a fireplace and ceiling fans, a sitting room and a living room. The kitchen was big and it had a center island with 3 hanging lights over it, and all the appliances were included. The cabinets were white and the countertops were a beige marble. We also had a deck, in addition to the patio, and also an enclosed porch which was my favorite.

Our house was on a Cul de sac and our address was going to be One Tupelo Lane. We loved it. Can you tell how excited I am? Billy was excited too. I was overwhelmed and started to cry and he looked at me and said, "Happy Tears?" I shook my head yes.

We went to the bank and applied for our mortgage and we were approved. In the meantime, we said nothing to family, not a word. I asked Billy if he was going to tell his parents and he said, "Yeah, I will invite them for dinner and give them a new address. That is, if you are ok with it." I said, "Of course it is. I am not going to hold a grudge for the rest of my life. I am not that kind of person." He said, "You gonna tell your parents?" I said, "Yup, I am gonna invite them for dinner too." I laughed and said, "Well now I will be able to invite them down and they will have a room." He said, "Your brothers and their wives will have rooms too." I told him we had a lot of work to do before we invited anyone and he agreed. He said, "We need to buy some stuff, you know like a dining room set and some sitting room furniture and outdoor furniture. I want to make it nice before I invite anyone over." He paused for a second and said, "I am not going to say anything at the office either." I shook my head and said, "Yeah, it's nobody's business but ours."

We continued to work and go out to dinner, and just being ourselves, while we were waiting for closing date, but we did not say anything to anyone. It was our little secret and it was fun keeping it. Once we closed on the house, I told Billy that we would have to let Human Resources know because we had a different address. He said, "Oh. Yeah, forgot about that." I said, "But that doesn't mean anyone else has to know, just Human Resources. It's up to you." He agreed.

We were notified of our closing date and of the closing costs, which we agreed to pay. We had the money in the bank, so we were all set. Closing Day was here and we got the cashier's check, did our walk through and then headed to the lawyers office to sign our lives away. It was a little scary, but we ended up being fine. We walked out about an hour later with keys to our new home. Billy took a selfie of us, smiling ear to ear, with our new home behind us and he was holding the keys. It was a great picture. I said, "That is how we should tell everyone. Just send them the picture." He smiled and said, "Yeah?" I said, "Yeah, why not?" He said, "I love this picture. I want to get it enlarged and framed and hang it in our living room or sitting room or some room." He started laughing. And he did and it was a great picture. We hung it in the hallway as you enter our side door from the enclosed porch. We put a shoe tray and coat rack and key holder in there.

We decorated the whole place with new furniture and decorations and it took us a few months and still we didn't tell anyone what we were doing. We visited his parents and my parents in between doing the house and they had no clue. They didn't ask to visit either, so we just left it like it was. We wanted to finish with decorations and furniture and have everything the way we wanted before anyone was invited and we were almost done.

We did end up going to California for a little vacation and we went to my parents in Connecticut for the Fourth of July and now it was August. Billy and I decided that we would have a big picnic out back and have a house warming party and we were almost ready to announce it. We were busy working and buying the last few things for our new house and then planning the party and buying things for that. We decided to have the party catered because it would just make things easier.

Billy and I made a lot of money together, but we were smart with it. We didn't overspend on anything and only bought what we needed and found good sales. We were very comfortable as far as money goes and we still saved every week. We had a nice cushion.

9

THE PARTY

We decided to take some vacation time around the party so we could get things set up for our big surprise. We took 2 weeks vacation and we sent out the invitations for a house warming picnic party. We used the picture of us in front of the house with Billy holding the keys on the front of the invite. We invited our friends, our families and our work family. It was going to be about 50 people give or take. We even made party favors, which were little sipper bottles of booze with a shot glass for each person, wrapped up in netting.

We had also decided on a date to get married, but Billy and I decided that we did not want a big wedding. We knew his mother was going to put up a fuss, but we didn't care. We wanted to have a very small wedding with just family and a couple of friends and just have a very small reception.

We were not going on a honeymoon right away because we bought the house instead. We did things OUR way. They may have been backwards to everyone else, but it was fine for us. It was what WE wanted to do. We were going to announce our wedding date at the picnic, which would be April 18 next year.

We had already picked out the restaurant where the reception would take place and we put a deposit on it. Billy and I picked the church and set that up. If anyone in the family wanted to do anything else, like flowers, extra food, etc. They were welcome to it, but we were getting married in THAT church and have the reception at OUR restaurant and we picked our food.

We had already made our list of guests and I ordered the invitations and we were going to mail them out after our house warming.

A couple days went by after we sent out the invites and his mother called him. "Billy? What the hell is going on? You bought a house?" We were sitting in the same room when he took the call and he told me it was her calling. He looked at me, covered the speaker and whispered *"YUP, Here it comes."* I snickered. He said, "Yes, we did. We bought a house and that's why you got an invitation to come and see it." She was all upset because she didn't know about it. "How come you didn't tell me Billy?" He laughed and said, "Ma, nobody knew about it, just me and Em. We have been working hard for months to get it just the way we wanted, before we invited anyone to see it." She was so flustered. "You bought it months ago and you didn't tell me?" He laughed again. "That's right mom. No one knew about it, just me and Em. Is there a problem with that?" She was quiet and I think she knew at that point, she was starting trouble. She was fumbling for words. "Um.. no, it's ah, not a problem, umm. I mean, I am ahh shocked that you, ahh didn't tell anyone. That's all." Billy told her that our business was OUR business and that if we didn't want to tell anyone, we didn't have to. "NO ONE, and I mean no one knew until we sent out the invitations. Are you coming or what?" She was still fumbling and she knew she better be careful what she said to him. "Umm. Yeah, I mean, yeah, should I bring something? Are you ok?" Billy said, "Mom, I am fine. I am doing very well and Em is fine too, in case you wanted to know, and no you don't need to bring anything except Dad." She thanked him and hung up. He hung up and started laughing. "She is a piece of work and she better not start anything at this party or I will be kicking someone's butt." I laughed.

A couple days after that, we received a lot of calls congratulating us and RSVPing saying they would be coming and asking what we need.

My parents called and they were so happy and shocked. My mom said, "OMG, from the picture in the background, it looks gorgeous. We can't wait to see it. Congratulations to both of you. We are sooo sooo happy for you both. What can we bring? Is there anything you would like or need as a house warming gift?" We thanked her and told her she didn't need to buy anything or bring anything. My mom said, "I know you won't do what I tell you to, so I am going to just make a suggestion." She laughed and then said, "You should make a registry of things that you need and you can use it for your wedding too. Just a suggestion."   I told her that I loved her idea and that I would talk to Billy about it. He actually loved it, so we went to do a registry of gifts for the party and for the wedding. I told my mom, dad and brothers to come a few days before the party and that we had room for all of them to stay.   We sent the registry to everyone and told them that they did not need to bring a gift, but of course, they all did.

The party was in a couple of days and mom and dad showed up, along with my brothers and sisters-in-laws, and Billy and I were setting everything up and getting ready. We had a bunch of folding tables and tablecloths and folding chairs and we set them all up. We rented round tables and folding chairs for eating and used the long folding tables for the food. We set up the enclosed porch, the patio, the pool area and the kitchen and dining area for people to sit and eat as well.

Billy had a friend that was a bartender and he hired him for the day. Billy had him set up in the corner under the overhang with his own table and coolers. We had balloons and flowers on all the tables and we had a small table with all the party favors.

The party went off without a hitch and everyone had a good time, even Billy's mom. I could tell she was still upset that she didn't know about the house and she didn't know what Billy and I had planned. She was so nosey and wanted to know everything that was going on. I heard of people like this, but never actually met one. I don't care to know anymore of them. They are annoying.

Anyway, we got some nice gifts and everyone loved the house and what we did to it. We had before and after pictures on a table so people could see what we did. My mom and dad were so proud of us and so were my brothers and sister-in-laws. Billy's sisters were really impressed and kept smiling at me. His dad kept hugging me and at one point, pulled me aside and hugged me and said, "I am so proud of you guys. You are the best thing that could have happened to him. I have never seen him this happy in all my life." I hugged back and thanked him and said, "Well at least one of his parents thinks that." He laughed and said, "I know that she can be a pain in the ass and most of the time she is, but she likes you. She is just very protective of her son." I told him it's time that she lets go. "He is a grown man now and doesn't need mommy looking after him. It's my job now." He said, "You and I know that, but now we have to convince her." He laughed and then said, "Just ignore her."

His southern accent was so cool. It was a bit more than what Billy had and he was a little bit hard to understand, so I really had to listen when he talked to me.

He was a really nice man and Billy definitely took after him in the personality area. They were both happy go lucky and not much bothered them. I have never seen Billy get really mad, but I did see him upset. I saw his father get mad that day when he hit the countertop in the kitchen, but that was it and he apologized for losing his temper in front of me.

Everyone was happy to get their little party favors and thought it was a great idea. Most people opened it up and drank the shot before leaving. We had a few tipsy people, but no one really got drunk, drunk. Thank God.

We announced our wedding date at the picnic and told everyone that the invites would be mailed out next week. We only had one person in the crowd that wasn't happy. Guess who that was? OMG. The fucking drama that she errs is unbelievable. I told Billy that I didn't know if I was ever going to have a good relationship with her. He told me it would blow over and I told him that there was nothing to blow over. I never did anything to her or said anything to her that would make her act like this. He shrugged his shoulders and I knew he didn't want to take a side and of course, I never expected him to. It was his mother and she would always be his mother and nothing was going to change that. He kissed me and knew that I understood. I hugged him and he said, "I know you guys don't get along and there is really nothing I can do to make that change, but I will NEVER, ever let her be mean to you. I will not tolerate that shit and if it comes down to picking between you and her, you know it will be YOU. It will always be you Em. And further, I will let her know this ahead of time." I hugged him so tight and said, "Good to know Babe but I would never expect you to <u>have</u> to choose." He looked shocked at me and said, "You didn't know that already?" I told him that I <u>did</u> know, but it was nice to hear it.

He said he was happy that she didn't start any shit at the party, but he thinks his father put the fear of the Lord in her. He laughed. I laughed with him and said, "She asked me why we picked out the wedding invitations without her and I told her that we picked them out together and we didn't need any help." He looked shocked at me and said, "WHAT? She started on you when I wasn't looking?" I shook my head and said, "It was nothing. I put her in her place and I plan on doing it whenever it's needed. I will let you know if I need any help." He shook his head and said, "What the fuck am I gonna do about her?" I laughed and said, "I have her under control, now that I know what she's like. Be ready though, because when she gets the invite and finds out we picked out the church and restaurant and the food without her, she is gonna freak out." He frowned and said, "Isn't that usually what's on the invite though?" I said, "Yup, but I told her it was a Save the Date to eliminate any party day problems." I laughed and he started belly laughing. "OMG, you really DO know how to get around her." I shook my head.

We started cleaning up the party and my mom and everyone was pitching in and everyone else went home. My brothers were walking around with trash bags and my sister-in-laws had the paper towels and windex and they were cleaning all the chairs and tables that we rented because they would be picked up in the morning. Me and Billy were folding them up and my dad was helping carry them to the garage. Everyone was busy and before you know it, we were done and cleaned up.

My mom pulled me aside and said, "I don't know if I should say anything or not, but it's been bothering me, so I am just gonna say it." I looked at her and said, "What's wrong ma?" "It's Anna. She is a little weird, don't ya think?

And she has been saying stuff to all your guests all day and normally, I wouldn't give a shit, but when your name is involved, it's my business." I had a shocked look on my face and said, "What the fuck did she say Ma? Tell the truth." She said, "Well, first I saw her talking to Billy's sisters and she mentioned your name and said something like, 'she is using him' and then she was talking to one of your co-workers and she said, 'yeah, I don't think this will last long and she is using my son' and then she was talking to Dad and she said, 'don't you think this is all too soon, I mean buying a house and getting married after only knowing each other a couple of months?' Dad was shocked that she was saying it and said, 'Personally, I don't think it's anyone's business but their own and I keep out of my daughter's business. She is an adult and I think she knows what she is doing.' He told me all that and after listening to her talking to everyone about you, I am pissed at her." I told my mom that I was pissed now too and thanked her for telling me and told her that if she heard anything else to let me know.

That did it. This topped the table and I was not going to let this slide. She was now on my SHIT LIST. You never want to be on my shit list and she was going to learn that. I went to Billy and told him what happened and what my mom told me. He was steaming and said, "I will fix her ass right now. Who the hell does she think she is? She is now UNINVITED to our wedding and I mean it. I do not want her there. He went into the house and got the invitations, which were not sealed yet and we still had to put them together. He found their envelope and crossed off Mrs. so that the envelope read Mr. Daniel Emerson. I said, "Billy, don't do that because you will regret it later when you cool down." He was MAD. This was the first time I saw him mad. He said, "Even when I cool down, I DO NOT want her at my wedding. This is FUCKING BULLSHIT. NO, she is not coming."

I walked away because I didn't want to upset him anymore than he already was. I went outside and I was sitting by the pool with my family and I told them what he did and how mad he was. My mom said, "I hope I didn't start a whole family feud. That was not my intention, but I didn't like what she was saying about you." I said, "Mom, you did the right thing by telling me. That is just not right what she did. I never did anything to that woman for her to hate me like she does." I started to cry and Jesse handed me a tissue and my dad came over to console me. Billy came out and apologized to everyone for his mother's behavior and told them that she was uninvited to the wedding and he would not be changing his mind about it. He sat next to me and told me not to worry about anymore problems. He said, "I called her and I told her she was uninvited to our wedding and that she was no longer welcome at my house and that I would no longer be coming to her house. She was crying and apologizing and I told her to go to hell. I am done with her shit and she is not going to ruin my life. My father warned her and she didn't give a shit so maybe now she will." He hugged me and said, "It's over Em. It's over and I don't want you to cry or be sad about it, because you did nothing to her and she is treating you like shit and I will not allow that. You are the love of my life and she is not going to take you away from me or make you walk away from me because of her."

My mom got up and went over to hug him and said, "I didn't mean to start anything, but I hated to hear her badmouthing my daughter and I won't allow that." Billy hugged my mom and said, "You didn't start anything ma, she did, and I just ended the whole fucking thing. I'm done." Billy's phone was ringing and it was his Dad's number. He answered the phone in front of my family and he sat back in the lounger chair. "Hi Dad." His dad was talking to him, but he didn't have it on speaker. Billy said, "Yes, I did and I am not changing my mind Dad. I am done with her shit. You warned her and I warned her and she was talking shit about Emily during the whole party to my co-workers and to Emily's Dad. I will not tolerate that. Emily is a good woman and I love her and nothing about that is going to change. She couldn't get that through her head, so she is out of my life and I mean every word." His father was talking to him and then

Billy said, "She already had 4 chances and she blew them all. I'm done Dad. I am not going to let her ruin my life with Emily. I will still keep in contact with you and you can visit, but I do not want her here and I will never come to your house again. My sisters and their husbands are also welcome to come and visit but I repeat, I will never come to your house again."

There was a pause and he said, "Don't be upset Dad. Nothing is changing between you and me, I promise you, but I want nothing to do with her anymore." They went back and forth for a few more minutes and then Billy said, "Ok Dad, talk to you soon." He looked at me and said, "My dad is upset, but he will be ok. I will make sure I keep in close contact with him so he doesn't feel like he did anything wrong. He is really pissed at my mom."

I had tears welling up in my eyes and I felt so bad for his dad. He was such a nice man and I couldn't believe that he married such a fucking bitch and put up with her all these years. I didn't say any of this to Billy, I was just thinking it. I think my mom knew what I was thinking because she smirked at me and I smirked back. God, I was so glad that Billy took after his Dad. He was nothing like his mom and didn't look like her either. His sisters took after her in the looks department but I think they all had their dad's personality.

I knew that I/we would be getting phone calls from his sisters wanting to know what happened because after all, she would tell them a different story than what actually happened and make me look like the bad guy.

It didn't take long and the phone calls started. First it was Sarah and she talked to her brother and then Liz called me to find out, but Liz told me she didn't believe a word that came out of her mouth. She and I were buddies and she told me that she overheard her talking to one of our co-workers and telling them that the marriage wouldn't last long and that I was using him.

This is fucking great and now I had to figure out who she told this to, so I could explain what was going on, or maybe I would just leave it up to Billy because it was his mother that started all this fucking shit. She really was a piece of shit for starting all this crap. I told Billy what Liz said and he told me what Sarah said and Sarah overheard her talking too. He told me he would take care of the co-workers and not to worry about anything and he would straighten everything out. "I will tell them what a piece of shit my mom is. Don't worry." He started laughing to make light of the whole situation, but I knew he was really upset over it. The co-workers that we invited were the owners, Kaufmann and Smith, my paralegals, Mia, Ginny and Evelyn, the new attorney, Pam Sanders and her secretary, Linda Bartone and another attorney that Billy was friendly with. I was more concerned with Attorney Kaufmann and Attorney Smith and hopefully she didn't say anything to them.

And here we thought that the party went off without a hitch. Ha-Ha. The joke was on us and I thought I had a handle on this bitch.

Well, now she was gonna suffer for what she did. I still can't believe she did that. I felt bad for Billy though, because it IS his mom and he had to choose between me and her and it really isn't fair that you have to do that. I really did feel bad for him, but I didn't make him choose. He did it on his own and his mom is who caused it, not me.

So we had another week off before going back to face the music. My parents stayed another day and then we took them to the airport and my brothers left the day after the party. We decided to hang by the pool and hot tub and enjoy our new house that was all finished and just the way we liked it. We put all the invitations together and I asked Billy again if he wanted to change his mind and he took the invite and sealed it up and we mailed it out with just his father's name on it. All the invites were mailed out and we were done. My mom wanted to order the flowers and we approved that and they wanted to pay for the rehearsal dinner, but Billy said his dad and sister's were paying for it and thanked them for offering.

We went back to work the following week and Billy said to just wait and see if anyone says anything first. We worked the whole week and no one said a word to us about her little remarks but they did say what a nice party it was and that they loved our house.

Billy decided to call a small meeting with just the people we invited to the party and we all met in Conference Room A. He told them that he wasn't sure who his mom talked to, but he was informed that she did talk to a few people in the room. He said, "I don't know exactly what she said, but I do know that she did talk to some of you here and she did not have anything nice to say about Emily. This has been an ongoing thing with her and I am not sure why, but I wanted to apologize for her behavior here in public before all of you. If she didn't talk to you, you can leave and I would appreciate it if you didn't say anything to anyone about it."

Pam, her secretary and my 3 paralegals left the meeting, along with the Attorney that was Billy's friend, and the two owners stayed. Oh fucking wonderful….

Attorney Kaufmann said to Billy, "Billy, you shouldn't worry about little incidents like this

one. There will be so many more in your life.
She talked to me, but she didn't get very far
because I told her how much I liked Emily and
that she was a good employee and I had no
idea what she was talking about and she
moved on to the next person, which was
Attorney Smith here." Attorney Smith said,
"She started talking to me too, but I told her
that she was wrong about Emily and that
everyone that met her, loved her and we all
thought she was a terrific person and she
should think so too and she moved away from
me too. Don't let her get to you Billy. It
sounds like she is looking for attention is all."
Billy told them that she was uninvited to the
wedding and that he cut all ties with her. "I
don't want her bad mouthing my Emily and
she has caused enough trouble already. I
apologize for her behavior, and I hope you all
had a good time at the party." They both said
the party was wonderful and they
congratulated us again on our beautiful house.

10

A FAMILY SURPRISE

We started to leave the room and then I remembered that I wanted to nominate Evelyn for Top Team Player for the month. I had forgotten to nominate her last December when all hell broke loose and I felt bad. I spoke with both of the owners and told them what an awesome job she did and that she never complained, not once while we were so overwhelmed with work and that she put in overtime everyday to get her work done. They both agreed that she should win the award for the month. The summer months were difficult in the office too, because everyone was taking vacation days and the other paralegals had to cover for them. They did give the award to her and she was so grateful to me for nominating her. Billy also put in a nomination for her because she helped him too. They made a big deal over the award and called an office meeting to announce her. She had tears in her eyes and came to hug me before she left the meeting.

Months went by and Christmas was coming. I called my mom and asked if they would like to come here for Christmas instead of us flying there. She said they both would love to, but Jack and Izzy had other plans and Jesse and Maria would probably come. I asked what Jack was doing because he was always there for Christmas. She said, "I can't tell you. I am sworn to secrecy". I frowned and said, "Ok? That's weird ma."

I asked Billy if he wanted to invite any of his family for Christmas and he said, "Nope. I'm good. Are your parents coming?" I felt bad, and I left it alone and just said, "Yeah and Jesse and Maria, but Jack and Izzy have other plans that my mom said she can't tell me because she is sworn to secrecy. Isn't that weird?" He looked at me and said, "Really? Yeah, that IS weird." He came up behind me and grabbed me and said in a spooky voice, *"What do you think it is? What is going on*?" I laughed and turned around and said, *"I don't know"* I tried to sound spooky, but it didn't come out that way. He laughed at me. He picked me up and carried me to the bedroom and fueled the fire and kept fueling it over and over and we made love in the middle of a Saturday afternoon and it was wonderful.

We really loved our home and we went all out decorating it for Christmas. We decorated every single room downstairs, even the bathroom. We even decorated the bedrooms that my parents and brother would be staying in. Not overdone, just a few things to get in the Christmas Spirit and some mistletoe in the doorways. I put my brother's favorite whiskey on the dresser with a couple of shot glasses and we bought fancy towels and washcloths and put them in the bathrooms for my parents and brother and sister-in-law. I wanted it to be special. It was my mom's favorite holiday too and she was away from home, so I made it extra special. I put a bottle of Amaretto on their dresser with glasses, because that was their favorite.   We even had 14 inch lighted Christmas Trees on the night tables for both of them.

We had lights inside and outside and Billy bought a blow up Santa with reindeer for out on the front lawn. He had a blow up Christmas Tree floating in the pool out back and we put a Christmas Tree in the enclosed porch and in the sitting room and in the living room. The house was big, so it didn't look overdone. I loved it and it was our first year having Christmas in the house, so I was going to do what I wanted. Billy and I both loved Christmas and it was our favorite holiday. Not to mention that we would be engaged for a whole year on Christmas Day. We were so excited to entertain or should I say, I was. I think he was a little sad, but he never said he was. It's been 4 months since he broke ties with his mom. I wonder if she feels bad for what she did and said? We were putting lights on the tree in the porch and I said, "Billy?" He turned to me and said, "Yeah?" I said, "If you need to change your mind, it is ok with me. I don't want to keep you away from your family and it's making me sad." He pulled me close to him and said, "I don't want you to be sad. I am NOT sad. I am still MAD. If I change my mind, I will let you know first ok? Relax. I am fine." He kissed me with those hot lips and fueled the fire and I teased him and told him not to start a fire in the porch. He laughed and said, "Why? No one can see if we start a fire out here." I laughed at him and we ended up going to the bedroom again. That bedroom saw a lot of action, not to mention our walk-in shower and the sitting room and the living room and the pool and the hot tub and the……. Well, you get the picture. LOL.

My mom and dad came first and my brother came a few days later. Everyone was hush hush about Jack and Izzy and I kept asking what was going on and no one would tell me. I was starting to get mad about it and I said to my mom, "How come everyone knows about Jack except me? Aren't I part of this family anymore?" My dad said, "Yes of course you are honey, but Jack asked us not to say anything and we have to honor his wishes." I was sad because I felt like I didn't belong to the family anymore and I told everyone that. My mom and Jesse were sad but they said they couldn't tell. What the hell was going on that they couldn't say anything to me? I don't get it. I saw my Dad go upstairs with his phone and my mom followed him. Jesse was talking to Maria and I offered them a drink and I put out some appetizers to pick on. Billy was the perfect host. He got along so well with Jesse and my parents. We all sat in front of the fireplace in the living room talking and Jesse commented on the bedroom and said it was tastefully decorated and they loved it, along with his whiskey. Billy said, "That's your sister's doing. She wanted everything perfect and she did a great job." Jesse and my parents were well aware of the shit that was going on between Billy and his mom, so they never asked any questions about it and for that, I was thankful. We all had a great time. Christmas Eve was tomorrow and we decided to take everyone out to dinner to our favorite restaurant, named the Hawthorne & Wood. Billy asked everyone if he could do some of the ordering and if they trusted him and everyone agreed. He ordered all the appetizers for everyone and they were really pleased. They all ordered their own dinners after that and they loved the food here. Billy and I came here a few times to celebrate certain things and we thought my parents and my brother would appreciate it and they did.

When we got home, my parents ran upstairs and they seemed excited about something and Jesse and Maria said they wanted to go bring the gifts down. I looked at Billy and said, "Something is going on. I wonder what's happening?" Billy said, "They are acting weird for sure." Jesse and Maria came down the stairs with my parents in tow, my mom was crying and my dad was holding up his phone and when he got to the bottom of the stairs, he handed me the phone. It was Jack and Izzy on FaceTime and Izzy was holding a baby. "WHAT THE FUCK?" Jack started laughing and said, "Surprise sis. We decided to have a baby before we got too old." I just opened my mouth in shock. I didn't even know she was pregnant. I couldn't talk. Billy and I just looked at each other. I had a hard time saying congratulations. "Oh My God, Is this for real? You guys had a baby? CONGRATULATIONS." And the tears came flowing down my face. "How come this was a secret? Why didn't you want me to know?" Jack said, "Em, we wanted to surprise you for Christmas. Izzy literally just had her by cesarean and we had it scheduled for tonight. IT'S A GIRL and she is beautiful. Her name is Haley Hannah West." I still couldn't believe this. "Awww. Jack, you gave her mom's name as a middle name. That is so sweet. I love you guys, but I don't like that you kept this as a secret. How did you manage to keep this from me for nine friggin months? I was there in July." He said, "Yeah, she wasn't showing in July. She was only 3 months. Ha-ha."

They showed the baby to everyone all around on the phone and then they hung up. I glared at my mom and she said, "Honey I had to keep it a secret. Jack and Izzy asked me to." All I could say was, "When did they change their mind about having a baby? I thought it was set in stone." She told me that Izzy was having second thoughts about not having one and she was working on Jack to change his mind and he did. Well, it certainly <u>was</u> a surprise. I looked at Billy and said, "I am an auntie and you are an uncle." He smiled at me and said, "Yeah, wow. This is awesome."

Then I pointed to my parents and said, "You guys are GRANDPARENTS." We all cheered and we poured some shots and celebrated Haley Hannah West, coming into the world on Christmas Eve.

I was still mad and when Billy and I were getting into bed, I said, "My family is weird. I guess everyone's family is weird. I just don't see how they could exclude me with this and how can they expect me to be excited? I mean it WAS a surprise, but really? This is not the kind of surprise you keep a secret. Do you think I am over-reacting?" He turned his head on his pillow to face me and said, "We both have weird families. I don't think you are over-reacting at all. That is not the kind of thing you surprise a family member with. I am on board with you there." I felt better that I was not the only one that thought it was weird. I laughed and said, "Ok, rant over. I will never speak of it again. Maybe." I laughed again and Billy laughed with me. "Come here beautiful. Let's light a fire."

The next morning there was hustle and bustle downstairs and Billy was gone from the bed. I went down in my robe and he was busy making coffee and French Toast. I grabbed him and planted a big kiss on him. "Merry Christmas you handsome man. I love you so much" He picked me up and said, "You wanna start a fire, right here in the kitchen next to the stove?" We laughed and he put me down. "Merry Christmas, beautiful. I love you more than you know." He was hugging me so tight.

My parents, Jesse and Maria came down the stairs and everyone was in their robes and we all hugged and wished each other Merry Christmas. Me and Maria set the dining room table and my mom was serving coffee and everyone was putting stuff on the table. We had a nice breakfast together and I didn't mention anything more about Jack, Izzy and the baby. I think everyone was avoiding the subject. Why can't everyone just be truthful and get along without hiding shit? I think Billy knew I was still upset about it, but he said nothing. I should have had Christmas with just Billy and we wouldn't have to tiptoe around.

Billy and I were making a rib roast with all the trimmings and Maria and Mom pitched in to help with the cooking. Jesse and my dad were watching a football game on TV and my Dad loved the Big Screen.

I broke the silence and said, "Did anyone talk to Jack and Izzy today and see how everything is going? I want to see that baby's face again. OMG. She is so cute." My mom's face lit up and she said, "Oh, Let's call now and see." My dad got them on FaceTime and we got to see the baby and she was awake. Izzy was sore but they had her on pain killers. Jack was a totally different person and I couldn't believe he was a dad. He was holding the baby and you could see the love he had for his daughter. I never in a million years pictured him with kids. Probably because he swore up and down he would never have one.

So Christmas was a success and everyone had a good time. My mom was in her glory that we were all around her, even though Jack and Izzy were off being parents and she wasn't at her own house. She told me that she appreciated the fact that I made it special for her, so I knew she noticed.

Everyone stayed a few days after Christmas and then left for Connecticut and they made it home safe.

11

OH ANNA! SUCH DRAMA

I heard through the grapevine, (Liz) that Billy's mom did not have her big bash for New Year's Eve and she didn't want anyone sleeping over and she didn't cook for New Year's Day. Liz said she was super depressed and no matter what they all did, she wouldn't snap out of it. I knew right then and there, that it was up to me to stop this shit. I didn't feel guilty or anything and she brought it all on by herself, but I had to stop it. I did not want Billy and his mom to be separated for life.

I called Billy's Dad and told him that I wanted to set up a lunch with just his mom and me at a restaurant nearby my house and asked if he would drive her because she did not drive. He agreed and I set it up.

I took a day off from work and the morning of the lunch, I told Billy that I set up a lunch with his mom and I took the day off and I told him I wanted him to go to work and leave it to me. He argued with me and told me not to, but I told him that he can't go through life like this.

He insisted that he go with me and I told him that it was just me and his mom and his father would be in the car. He was upset with me, but never raised his voice once. He went to work and kissed me on the cheek and said, "Good Luck with this. She is a pain in my fucking ass. I wish you didn't do this." I smiled at him and said, "It will be fine. She won't pull anything in the restaurant and if she does, I will snap back at her like an elastic." He laughed and he went to work.

I drove to the restaurant and his Dad was there already and his mom saw me drive in and got out of the car. I parked near their car and got out. I grabbed her hand and said, "How have you been Anna?" She looked shocked that I was being so nice to her. She said, "Not good Emily. Not good." I walked with her into the restaurant and I gave my name and we were taken to our table. She said, "You made reservations?" I told her I did because I wanted a table in the corner away from people.

I ordered a margarita and she got one too. I said, "Let's order some food and talk while we are eating. I want to talk to you calmly and softly and I don't want you to make a scene about anything. Is that understood?" She shook her head yes. We ordered some lunch and while we were waiting I said, "Anna, you <u>do</u> know what you did, right? Do you understand why Billy and I are mad at you?" She shook her head yes. I continued and said, "Why did you feel the need to berate me in front of my family and friends at my house party? Why would you do that to me? Have I ever done anything to you or said anything to you that would make you hate me like you do?" She shook her head no and then said, "I don't hate you at all." I said, "Anna, if you don't hate me, why are you telling everyone that I am using your son and that the marriage won't last? Why on earth would you say stuff like that? Tell me the truth Anna. I need to know why you feel that way about me." She put her head down.

The waitress brought our food and we started to eat and I gave it a rest for a few minutes. I needed to get to the bottom of this shit. I took

a few bites of my bacon burger and said,
"Mmm. This is delicious. How is your food?"
She said, "It's really good. Thank you for this.
I appreciate it." She took a sip of her
margarita and so did I. She said, "I am so
sorry. I felt like you were taking my son away
from me. I don't know why I felt that way, but I
did. I felt that you were taking advantage of
him because he is a lawyer and makes a lot of
money. You left your apartment and went to
live with him and he was paying for everything
for you and now he bought a house." I looked
at her and tilted my head and said, "Really
Anna? That's what you think is happening
here? Well, let me straighten things out for
you right here and now. I moved out of my
apartment and moved in with Billy and we split
the rent. I paid for half of it and I bought all the
groceries. When we left the apartment, we
both picked out the house and we both pay for
the mortgage and we both split the bills. You
see Anna, I am a paralegal and I make a lot of
money too. Actually, almost as much as Billy
and we are doing very well together. I love him
with all my heart and even though he proposed

to me after 3 months of knowing each other, it has been over a year that we have been engaged and we are still going strong. We still love each other more than you know. All this stuff I have just told you is really none of your business. It's our business, but just to straighten things out in your head, I told you. But in the future, we won't be telling our business to anyone, Anna, not even you because it is OUR business. If your daughters tell you their business, that is fine with me, but I will not be sharing that information with you or your husband or your family. If Billy wants to share information, that is his business and I won't stop him. He did not want me to come here today to talk to you, but I don't want all this to come between you and him and I hate it and I know you are suffering for what you did and said and I hate that too. I am not a bad person Anna. I am a good person and I want everyone to get along with each other. I did not start all this shit Anna. You did. You started it and I want it to end because I want Billy to be happy and I want you to be happy. Can't you see that?" She looked up at me and smiled and said, "I can see it now Emily. I guess you just told me off and I deserved all of it. I didn't really want it to come to this. I miss my Billy every single day and I apologize for everything I did and said. I really do feel bad for everything and I want it to stop and I promise that I will never let this happen again." I looked at her and said, "Do you swear that you will never badmouth me again, ever? Do you swear you will stay out of our business? Do you swear that you will tell me if you have a problem with me?" She smiled and said, "I swear, I swear, I swear for all three and more. Can you please forgive me for everything?" I told her that I forgave her but now she had to talk one on one with Billy because he was upset that she did all that to me.

Little did everyone know, that I recorded everything on my phone. I got the whole lunch recorded so I could play it back for Billy. Hopefully it worked because I never did anything like that before. I kinda of felt guilty for doing it, but I needed him to hear what I said and her answers.

I ordered a couple of mini sundaes for dessert and she smiled at me the whole time and said, "I really got you wrong Emily. You are a sweetheart and I can see why Billy loves you so much." I smiled back at her and said, "I am happy you can see that I am not a bad person." She said, "I never thought you were a bad person, only that you were taking my son away and I see that you are not trying to do that now." I tilted my head and said, "How so? I mean, did you think I was going to drive away with him and you would never see him again? I don't understand." She said, "I don't know what I thought. Maybe that you would change him and keep him away from family? I really don't know what I was thinking, but it was stupid and I am so sorry."

We finished our lunch and I walked her back to the car where Billy's father was taking a nap. He woke up and looked at both of us and smiled. She thanked me for lunch and the meeting and they left. I drove home.

I checked my phone when I arrived to see if the whole conversation was recorded on the app I downloaded and it was. Yay. I can let Billy listen if he wants to.

I noticed that he had texted me a few times but I had my phone on silent while we were at lunch. I texted him back and told him lunch was good and I would explain more when he got home. He wanted to take me out to dinner, so I got ready and he would be home in an hour. I freshened up and waited. I wasn't really hungry, but I knew he was. I just ordered a drink and an appetizer and I was good to go. I told him I recorded everything and he just stared at me and swallowed hard and said, "Um, you what?" I told him again, "I recorded the whole lunch Billy. I wanted you to hear your mother's answers and what I said to her." I sipped my drink and he was still staring at me. I said, "Are you upset with me?" He smiled and said, "No, of course not. I totally understand why you did it and I appreciate that you are trying to fix what my asshole mother caused." I looked at him lovingly and said, "It's killing me that you are not talking to your family, well, your mother, but you don't go to their house and they don't come here, so it's like the whole family. I don't want to be the cause of this and I hate it. I want you to be back the way you were with your family Billy." He smiled at me and said, "You were not the cause and you know it, and don't say it again. We all know who caused of all this shit." I smiled at him and said, "I just want things to go back the way they were and I want you happy." He said, "As long as I am with you, I am happy Em."

I gave him the ear phones and said, "Wanna hear what she said?" He took them and put them in his ears. The recording started when I parked the car. I saw him smiling a few times and then he was serious and then he was smiling. He was eating and listening and I was sipping on my second margarita. This was my 4th one today. Yummm. Margarita's!! I took one of his French fries and I was nibbling on it. He was smiling now and it didn't change. He listened to the whole lunch and took the earphones out and said, "Wow, That's what she really thought? Where the hell did she come up with this shit that you were stealing me away from her? She thought you were using me for my money? Dear God. My mother is a total idiot." I looked at him and said, "See, I told you that sometimes you just don't know what people are thinking and sometimes you will never know. I was surprised that she told me what she did and I am glad she explained what she was thinking. Stupid as it may seem." He said, "So now I need to talk to her?" I shook my head yes and I said, "Yes, In person and be nice Billy and be civil. Don't be calling her stupid or asshole or anything like that. She is your mother and she made a mistake. Be done with it." He smiled a loving smile at me and said, "I will. I will be nice." We finished up our dinner and we ordered a coffee, like we always do. He ordered a Beignet and of course, I had to eat one too, even though I was full. I smiled at him and he smiled back with the sparkles in those eyes. His love showed through his eyes every time he looked at me.

When we got home, we climbed into the shower for some fun and of course to get clean. We settled into the couch in the living room and we were snuggling when his phone rang. It was his mother. He looked at me and I said, "Answer it." He said, "I wanted to be the one to call her." I just looked at him and said, "Answer it Billy."

He picked it up and put it on Speaker Phone and said, "Hi Mom." She started crying. "I am so sorry honey. I really am. I was so stupid and I don't know what I was thinking. Can we meet up and talk?" He said, "Sure Ma, do you want to come over this weekend for dinner, you and Dad?" She said, "I was thinking, just you and me?" Billy said, "Yes Mom, it will only be you and me, but I want Dad to come for dinner too. I will figure out a place we can talk in private ok?" She seemed a little hesitant and said, "Ok." I said, "Anna? I will find a place that you and Billy can talk alone ok?" She said, "Ok honey. Thank you". They set it up for Sunday afternoon and I made a Taco Casserole. They both loved it last time I made it and it was a perfect meal to make ahead of time and just bake.

Sunday afternoon came and his parents showed up around 1:00, which was a lot earlier than I anticipated, but whatever. We weren't doing anything anyway and it would give him time to talk to his mom and I could sit with his dad.

Billy closed the sliding doors in the sitting room and blocked off the kitchen and living room and it made a nice little spot where they would be comfortable and could talk alone. I had bottles of water and some picky food like grapes and cheese and crackers on the coffee table to make it comfortable and inviting. I really did try to make this work. I reminded Billy when they drove up to keep his voice soft and talk to her calmly and not to call her names. He just smiled at me. "I am not a monster. She is." I just laughed at him and said, "Behave."

They hugged when she came in the door and she wouldn't let go of him. It took a minute. His Dad gave me a big hug and he and I went to the living room and Billy took his mom to the sitting room. Before he closed the slider, I peeked in and said, "Is this ok Anna?" She smiled at me and said, "Yes, dear. Thank you."

I went back to the living room and sat with his Dad, who already had a football game on the big screen TV. I said, "How has she been since our lunch?" He smiled at me and said, "I don't know what you said or did, but she has been totally different since that lunch. She is nicer to everyone, even me." And he laughed. "What DID you say to her?" I didn't want him to know that I recorded it, so I didn't tell him, but I just went over the important things that I said to her, as blunt as they were. He said, "She needed to hear all that. She doesn't realize how her words hurt people, but the words that her son said to her, hurt her bad and now she knows what it feels like." I told him how her words hurt me as well and she made me feel like I wasn't good enough for her son. He looked at me and said, "You are the best thing that has ever happened to Billy. I have never seen him so happy. He loves you to the moon and back Emily. When a man knows he found the 'one', he seals the deal." I smiled and told him I already knew that and I loved him more than anyone could ever imagine. "We were meant for each other, Dan and a woman knows when she has found the 'one' and that is why I said yes."

Billy and his mother were in the sitting room for an hour and a half. We could hear talking, but we couldn't make out what they were saying. It was civil and there were no loud outbursts. I thought I heard her crying at one point but wasn't sure and I hoped that it was guilt crying and not because Billy made her cry. I didn't think he would. He was a good man and I knew that or I wouldn't have said yes to his proposal.

They finally emerged from the sitting room and he had his arm around her shoulder and she was smiling, but looked like a child that had been scolded. They came into the living room and sat down and Billy said, "Everything is settled. Mom is going to be good from now on, Right ma?" Anna said, "Yes, I will be good from now on and I am very sorry for causing all this trouble. You have no idea how sorry I am Emily." I smiled and said, "Yes, I do Anna."

I got up and went into the kitchen and she followed me. "Can I help you do anything for dinner?" I said, "If you want to set the table you can. The dishes are here and the silverware is here." I pointed to both places. I set the oven for 375 and took the Taco Casserole out of the fridge and put it in the oven. I grabbed the napkin holder and put it on the table and started making a salad. Anna sat on the stool at the counter and watched me. "Did you cook or did Billy?" I said, "Actually, I cooked today. We usually take turns or cook together. It depends on what we are having. We usually prep together after shopping on Saturday, for the week. Billy likes to cook, so he does most of it, but I have some recipes that I like to make so I do those." She said, "That must be nice that you don't have to cook every night. I didn't have that luxury. Dan doesn't cook at all, but he likes to eat." She started laughing. She was really trying hard and making conversation and I was right there with her, trying to make it easier for her. I told her what I made and she said, "Oh that was good. Didn't you make that before?" I told her I had made it one time before and everyone loved it. I said, "Yesterday, I made Chicken Rollatini. Did you ever have that?"

She said she never tried it. I went into the fridge and took out a piece and warmed it up so she could taste it. She took a bite and looked at me. "Oh My God, Em. This is delicious. Can I have the recipe? Is it hard to make?" I told her it was pretty easy. She took a fork full into Dan and said, "You have to try this. It's Chicken Rollatini." And she shoved it in his mouth. Billy was laughing. "My Em is a good cook mom." Dan loved it, so I wrote the recipe down for her. She opened my fridge (being funny) and said, "What other delicacies do you have in here?" Then she closed it. I said, "Well, I made an ice cream cake for dessert. I think you will like that." She said, "For real? You made an ice cream cake? How do you do that?" I explained the process and she wanted that recipe too. Billy came in and said, "See what you missed mom? Emily is a good person and a good cook and she treats me good and she loves me and I love her." He hugged me from behind. She said, "I see what I was missing. Yes." I whispered to him in the hallway to stop reminding her of her fault. "It's over Billy, just leave it be and don't make her feel bad anymore. She is really trying." He agreed to stop.

We had a really nice dinner together. I made some homemade dinner rolls and we had that with the Taco Casserole and a salad. Anna helped me rinse the dishes and clear the table and I told Billy to go sit with his Dad and we would set up dessert. Even though he said it wouldn't affect his dad's relationship, it did and his dad missed him. I was so happy this shit was over. They both loved the ice cream cake and Anna couldn't stop talking about it.

12

YOU ARE MY FAVORITE EVERYTHING

We went back to work on Monday and people were in an out of my office and it seemed like everyone was back from winter vacations and they were all back to work because there were a lot of people buzzing around. Attorney Kaufman peeked in to say hi and asked me how things were going with the wedding and for a second, I forgot I was getting married. Oh My God, how could I forget? Oh, maybe the shit with his mother? LOL. I told him everything was all set and he came in and closed the door. I looked at him and said, "Is everything ok?" He smiled at me and said, "Yes, Of course. I know it's none of my business, but is everything ok with Billy's family? I know there was a little stink at the party and he told me his mother was uninvited. You don't have to answer if you don't want to. I was just concerned for him." I smiled and said, "Actually, this past weekend, everything was settled."   He smiled and said, "Excellent. I am glad to hear that." He got up and said, "If you ever need to vent or need an ear, I am right down the hall." I thanked him and he left. He was a nice man, but he was nosey. I didn't want to give him too much information. I just let him know everything was ok now.

I got to work and checked in on my ladies and they were all busy and I checked a few pieces of work they did and made a couple of suggestions. I also had to keep tabs on their education and make sure they were up to date with classes. Mia and Ginny were taking a course now and they were almost finished. Ev was all set and was up to date. I asked each one if they were comfortable, if they needed help with anything, if they had any questions or concerns and Mia just had one question which I took care of for her. They all seemed happy and Ev told me they were. She was my little spy. She told me everything and there really wasn't much to tell. They all got along and they shared work and helped each other. We all walked at lunchtime together and it was a nice getaway from our desks. We ate in the cafeteria and then went walking. Sometimes there were vendors in the building, so we always made sure to bring our wallets. I grabbed some nice stuff one day, like blankets

and books and baby things :) and I put it away
for birthdays or Christmas.

Billy and I also went shopping for baby Haley
and sent a huge box of gifts to Connecticut. I
couldn't wait to see her. They were going to
bring her to the wedding and I was so excited.

Valentine's Day was approaching and I wanted
to do something nice for my ladies. I gave
them each a gift certificate to have their nails
done and they each got a bouquet of flowers
delivered to them at the office and I took them
all out to lunch. I bought them donuts and
muffins and coffee for breakfast too. That
made them super happy and it made me
happy too.

Billy took me out for dinner on Valentine's Day
and bought me a beautiful heart shaped Ruby
and diamond necklace. It was a gorgeous
piece of jewelry and I kept thanking him over
and over. He really had good taste in jewelry.
He gave me the necklace in the restaurant and
then stood up and put it on me. He was such
a romantic. He even had roses on our table,
with a ribbon wrapped around the vase, at the
restaurant and he had flowers delivered to the

house. He stood back and said, "It's perfect. It looks beautiful on you."

He told me at dinner that he sent a bouquet of flowers to his mom too and I loved that he did that. He said he sent flowers to his secretary and gave her a gift certificate to Amazon.   I had something up my sleeve too. I bought him a gold chain and a cross. I also bought him a framed Valentine Sign that said, 'You're my Favorite.' My favorite pair of eyes to look into. My favorite way to spend an afternoon. My favorite person to laugh with. My favorite text to appear on my phone and always my favorite smile to see. You are my favorite everything."

He loved that sign and kept looking at it. He looked up at me and said, "I love you so much Em. You will never know how much. I am so happy you lost your car in that parking lot." I laughed and said, "I am glad you lost yours too".

We had a very romantic dinner that night and he finished it off when we got home by fueling the fire in the car, in the hallway and all the way to the bedroom and we left pieces of clothing from the door to the bedroom and he continued to fuel that fire until there was an explosion in there.

Our wedding was coming up fast and Anna made favors and chocolate for everyone. She asked if she could do it and Billy gave her the go ahead, which made her happy. Everything else was done and it was not fancy. Just the church, the ceremony, the restaurant reception, the flowers and favors and it was done. His parents paid for the rehearsal dinner the night before and my parents insisted on paying for the balance at the restaurant, so Billy let them. We ordered a DJ for music and he was really good. The wedding was beautiful and Billy was now my husband and I couldn't have been more proud. He held onto me the whole time and told me I was his queen and he was proud to have me as his wife. He treated me with the utmost respect and love and he would never tolerate any ill remarks against me by anyone and I mean anyone. His mother changed her tune after our meeting and her meeting with Billy. She was a completely different person after that. Liz was my inside spy and she said her mom never said a harsh word about me ever again.

Billy and I decided not to go on a honeymoon just yet because we bought the house. We had the money, but we didn't want to spend it just yet. We wanted a nest egg for emergencies and what not. It was the smart thing to do. We went away for a weekend after we were married, to Emerald Isle Beach and stayed for a few days and just relaxed by the water and in our beautiful romantic room with a hot tub. There were tons of things to do, but we didn't want to do any of them. We just enjoyed the beach and the pool and the hot tub and our room and then we drove home. It was very romantic and we both enjoyed the relaxation. We didn't tell anyone where we were going or even that we were going. We just disappeared.

Billy and I never discussed whether we wanted children. I wasn't opposed to having them, but he had never ever mentioned having them, even when my brother had Haley. He held her at the wedding and so did I and there was no real emotion over her from him. I decided I would ask him what his thoughts were on having kids. He said, "I am not gonna say I don't want kids, but I am also not gonna say I want them." He laughed and said, "Maybe I am not ready yet? I really don't know. How do you feel about it Em?" I told him I wasn't opposed to having them, but I wasn't sure if I wanted them at all. Maybe I wasn't ready yet either. He hugged me and said, "Let's leave the subject for a while and we will just wait and see what happens. I mean, we are not getting any younger, so if we decide to have children, it would have to be within the next few years. I don't want to be 40 when I have my first child.

Do you know what I am saying?" I shook my head yes and said, "Let's discuss it again in a year. I am 25 and you are 29, so we should really decide within the next year. Ok?" He kissed my cheek and said, "Deal." We didn't discuss it at all, but I was thinking about it, in a negative way. I really didn't think I wanted children and hopefully he says no too. Does this mean I am uncaring or unloving? No, it doesn't. It just means I don't think I can handle a child and actually I am afraid I wouldn't be a good mother. I don't want this to separate us and I would never let it. If he decides he wants a child, I would have one, because I love him and would do anything for him, but I don't want him to say he wants one, because he thinks I want one. This is so crazy and we really have to talk it out and make sure we are both on the same page.

13

BIGGER PROMOTION

So a year went by and we were still working at the same Law Firm and Billy was up for promotion to Attorney 4. Attorney Smith was talking about retirement and Attorney Kaufman was up for Managing Partner and they still needed another attorney to be a named partner. A lot of the attorneys under Billy had left the company to go other places and Billy was next in-line and he was wondering if he would make named partner. If he did, then the name would be Kaufman and Emerson, Law Firm. Billy was excited and I told him not to be too excited because we didn't have any idea what was going to happen or what they were thinking of doing. I knew that Attorney Kaufman liked both of us a lot and he took Billy under his wing and showed him the ropes and he knew Billy was a good attorney. This would mean a shit load more money for Billy, not to mention his name being on the door, the wall and everywhere else. Billy was like me, in that, he cared about people and their feelings. He treated his secretary and everyone in the office with the utmost respect and never spoke ill about anyone. He wanted to make sure everyone was happy and if they weren't, he wanted to know why and how he could help them. It's just the way he was. It was his personality and I loved him for that.

Attorney Smith named Billy the top Team Player for the month and I was wondering if that was a consolation for not naming him? Hmmm. I wonder what was going to happen. I didn't say anything to Billy about that. I just kept it to myself because I didn't want him to start getting nervous. I took him to Hawthorne and Wood for dinner and we celebrated his Team Player Award. They had a big meeting and gave him his award and check during the meeting. They always made a big deal about these awards. Team Player was a really big deal in this firm.

We constantly had meetings about it, but not too many people were interested in being a Team Player. Maybe because they didn't know how much they would be getting and I mentioned it to Attorney Kaufman. He said, "I would have people drooling around my office.

I don't want that. I want people to really care and to really be a Team Player because they want to, not just for the money." I understood that and said, "Ah Ok, Gotcha. I get it." He smiled at me and said, "I knew you would."

He asked me about Billy and his family and my family and how things were going. I was nice and just told him things were going very well. He shook his head and said, "Excellent. Glad to hear that."

Another month went by and Attorney Smith announced his retirement. He was 66 years old and said he and his wife were going to start traveling and all his birds had left the nest and he wanted to leave before they came back. He had everyone in hysterics. He was always cracking jokes and he was a super nice man and I was going to miss him. He had 6 children, 3 girls and 3 boys, well, now women and men. He was such a proud dad and everyone in the office knew what his children did for a living and he talked about them constantly. I loved that and I made sure to ask about his kids all the time.   After he made the announcement, he made another announcement, and we were all shocked. He named my Billy Emerson, the Managing Partner, not Attorney Kaufman. I instantly started crying and I saw Billy tear up.

Apparently, they didn't tell him before the meeting. Attorney Kaufman did not want the position and they gave it to Billy. They kind of asked him at the meeting if he would accept the position and of course, Billy accepted. So the name would be Emerson and Kaufman Law Firm. I was so friggin proud of him right now and he kept looking at me and he couldn't believe what he was hearing and neither could I. I was in shock, but I really think he was in more of a shock than I was. I'm so glad I remembered to put my phone on silent before entering the meeting. He texted me and said, "WTF? I fucking can't believe this. Why did Kaufman turn it down?" I texted back. "I am so fucking proud of you right now. We will talk later."

The meeting continued and lunch was brought in for everyone, courtesy of Attorney Smith and it wasn't just sandwiches, it was a full blown meal. Trays of food and salad and rolls and they were celebrating his retirement and Billy's promotion. Smith and Kaufman pulled him aside and they were talking and then they called me over. I walked over with my mouth full of food and hugged both owners and then my third owner. Attorney Kaufman explained that he would be retiring in a couple of years and that he was 63 years old, so he didn't want the position and wanted Billy to have it, so he would have a handle on everything by the time, he left. He told him it was a lot of work and a lot of responsibility and Billy told him that he was up for it. Normally, you have to put up money to become a partner and buy into it, but Attorney Smith said, "I am leaving my share in the company and it will become Billy's share, so he will not have to buy into it." Billy shook his hand and gave him a half man hug and said, "I am honored to take your position and you won't be sorry. I thank you for giving me your share. How can I ever repay you for this?" Attorney Smith smiled a big smile and said, "Take over and do a good job, like I know you will." Billy's salary was going to jump to $220,000 a year. Holy Shit and that was mid-grade pay, so he could go up from there. Attorney Kaufman had to bring in the clients and of course, Billy did too, but it was mainly Kaufman's job and he was really good at it.

A week later, they signed all the papers and Billy took over the month after that in July. His parents and my parents were over the moon happy for us and so proud of Billy. Every time I looked at him, I smiled with proudness. He did a really good job in his new position and he became everyone's favorite person in the office. He wasn't stern (and neither was Attorney Smith) and he made sure he made the rounds to everyone, every single day to say hi and find out if everyone was happy and if there was anything he could do for them. Everyone loved him so much, but not more than me.

He brought in the business that was expected of him and did so, more than Attorney Smith did and Kaufman was very proud that they picked him. Billy hired 4 more attorneys, because some of them had left the firm to go other places and he needed the help. He had the secretaries and he didn't want to let them go because they were good secretaries. We just spread out the work and had the other secretaries help out with some of the work load until the new attorneys started. I helped Billy with all that and everyone was happy. The office was running in tip top shape and we had a lot of work flowing through.

14

KIDS OR NOT?

A year had passed and it was time to talk about having a family. I told Billy that if he wanted to have a family, I would, but if he didn't, I was all set. He looked at me and said, "So, you are really saying that you don't want to have children?" I said, "Here is the thing Billy. If you want to have children, I will have them, because I want you to be happy and I don't want to split up over it. I am not saying that I don't want them. Actually, I am really scared, because I don't think I have the patience and I don't think I would be a good mom. I don't know if I was meant to have kids." He smiled at me and said, "Ok, phew. I was scared that you were gonna say, 'I want them' and I am having the same feelings about being a bad dad or not having the patience for it. Personally, I do not want a child and would rather we travel together. Does that sound bad? Does it sound selfish?" I smiled and hugged him and said, "Nope, not to me. I thought I was being selfish, but now that you say it, it doesn't sound like that at all." So, we got that out of the way and we both decided not to have children. I am sure this was not going to go over well with either of our parents, but I told him not to say anything and neither would I and we could avoid it that way. He laughed and said, "My mom already asked when we were gonna start a family." I looked at him and said, "She did? What did you say to her?" He laughed and said, "I just told her that we weren't sure if we were having any yet." I said, "And that shut her up?" He shook his head yes. I said, "Wow, she really did change." He wanted to know if my mom asked me yet and I told him she wouldn't dare ask me because she knows it's our business.

Billy and I also discussed whether I should stay on the pill or if he should have a vasectomy. He said that he didn't want me to have to continue to take a pill for the rest of my life, so he thought the best thing would be the vasectomy.

He wasn't too happy when he got home, but the ice packs helped and after a couple of days, he was back to normal. He would still have to be tested, according to his doctor, because he could have sperm in his semen for up to 3 months after the operation and I would still have to be on the pill. There is still the possibility that I could get pregnant, even after the vasectomy, so we had to be careful. He followed doctor's orders and was tested regularly until there was no more sperm. He even went an extra time to make sure and then I went off the pill. I didn't know this was such a big deal. I thought he just had the operation and it was a done deal, but it's not.

I ended up calling my mom and letting her know that we decided not to have children and Billy told her he had a vasectomy. She said she wasn't shocked because she had a feeling we weren't having them. Jesse wasn't shocked either and Jack was whatever. He didn't care either way and that is the way it should be. We all supported him when he said he wasn't having any. Not that he stayed with that decision, but whatever. Billy called his parents and had them on speaker and he told them that we were not having children and that he just wanted to let them know so they weren't expecting any news. His mother was upset, but she didn't start anything. Billy told her that this was a mutual decision and he told them that he had a vasectomy and that it was HIS decision, so there wouldn't be any misunderstandings. They were both understanding as far as I knew, but I would call my insider, Liz, later, and she would tell me if anything was said about me. I waited a couple of days and then called her. I said, "So has there been anything said about our decision?" She said, "What decision? What are you talking about?" I told her our news and she said, "OMG, no I didn't hear anything about it at all. Wow, I am so surprised my mom didn't get on the phone and start in." I was shocked and I said, "What do you think Liz? Are you surprised?" She said, "Are you kidding me right now? That is your friggin business and no one should have any opinion about it. You should know me by now hon." I thanked her and she said, "For what? Don't you dare. That is your business and I give you credit for standing up to her anyway. Besides, after the last thing she did, I don't think she will ever badmouth you again ever. That really did a number on her. My dad probably told her to keep her mouth shut and that's why I had no idea." She was laughing. She paused and then said, "We aren't having any either Em, but my situation is different. I can't have them and my mom knows already, but Sarah is going to have a few, so she says." I felt bad and said, "Oh Liz, I am so sorry. Are you ok?" She assured me she was ok.

I asked Billy if he knew she couldn't have any children and he said he knew and he forgot to tell me because we were going through all the shit with his mom and he didn't think it was the right time. He said, "I'm so sorry. I totally forgot to tell you. She had a tumor and had to have her uterus removed. They are both going to therapy for it and they are talking about adopting." I told him that she didn't mention anything about adoption. He said it was on the table, but maybe they changed their minds. I felt so bad and told Billy that this was important for me to know and he apologized again. I said, "She probably thought that I didn't care about her because she told me on the phone and I had no idea what was going on." He told me that she was in and out of the hospital in one day and that he sent her flowers and it was right after his mom pulled her shit at the party and he wasn't trying to keep it from me, but with all the shit that was going on, he meant to tell me and then forgot. He said, "Please don't be mad at me. I didn't do it on purpose. I will tell Liz that I forgot and she will understand" I told him I was not mad at him, but in the future, these kinds of things are important to know, no matter what was happening and he agreed.

15

HONEYMOON TIME

Billy and I were discussing where we wanted to go on vacation for our honeymoon. We both wanted to go overseas and we decided to go to Italy. We planned the whole trip and we even took some Italian lessons so we could speak some Italian and understand it. It was so much fun and it was better when two people were doing it together.

Once we were getting good at speaking Italian, we would say sexy things to each other and laugh. We had such a good time together. He would fuel the fire during the lessons and we would speak Italian and fuel the fire some more until we couldn't hold off anymore and… we either ended up in the shower, or the bedroom or wherever we were taking the lesson in the house. We still had a month to go before we left for Italy and we were getting excited. We were speaking Italian in the office to each other and our co-workers were laughing and thought it was cute. Everyone knew we were getting ready to go to Italy and they were excited for us.

So our honeymoon was here and we were all set to go to Italy. We were practicing how to say certain things and how to order food and talk to taxi drivers and we were in First Class and eating and drinking. We were in the air for about 8 1/2 hours, when all of a sudden, the flashing light went on overhead and the pilot got on the loud speaker and said that we were going to be hitting some heavy weather and we were expecting turbulence and to make sure our seatbelts were secure. Within seconds, I felt my heart hit my stomach and I got so scared. It felt like the plane was dropping fast in the sky. Billy held my hand tight and I looked at him and he had his eyes shut and he was squeezing my hand. I started praying silently and squeezed his hand back and then reached for him and we were hugging. The plane felt like it was bouncing and dropping. People were crying and screaming and luggage was falling out of the overhead bins and then the oxygen masks dropped and we put them on and we were still hugging each other so tight. I told Billy that I loved him over and over and he was saying it back to me. Our back packs were sliding around and he was trying to hold them in place with his feet. This went on for over a half hour and I thought we were going to die.

The pilot got back on the loud speaker and told us they were making an emergency landing and told us to put our head between our knees and keep our oxygen masks on and try to stay calm. Oh sure, stay fucking calm.

We were going to die and we were supposed to stay calm? The plane felt like it was falling out of the sky and it was complete and utter chaos on the plane with people screaming and crying. I was beginning to feel sick to my stomach with the plane falling so fast. Billy was still holding on to me and rubbing my back. "We are going to be ok, I just know it babe. We are going to be ok." All I could do was cry and I did not have the same feeling he did. I looked at the window and saw that we were close to the ground and then we hit. We hit hard and everything was flying all over the place, inside the cabin and the old man next to us was on the floor in the aisle and he was holding onto Billy's arm for dear life. Billy held onto him. We were on the ground, but we were sliding and I could see sparks and I heard sirens and saw fire trucks and we were still sliding. I guess the wheels didn't go down and the plane landed on its belly. It was so noisy with people yelling and screaming and crying. Billy was holding me tight. "We are ok Babe, we are ok, we are ok." The door opened and they were helping people down a slide and told us to leave our luggage and backpacks. Billy held me in his lap tight, as we slid down to the ground and people were there to help us as we hit the pavement. I was so weak from being scared, I couldn't stand up and Billy felt the same way, along with all the other passengers and we were all sitting on the pavement and we were being moved away from the slide so the other passengers could slide down. Billy never let go of me the whole time, not even for a second. He kept asking me if I was feeling ok and telling me everything was going to be fine.

Apparently we were somewhere in the UK. We were taken to a room in the airport and we collected all our luggage and backpacks and everyone was being checked out medically to make sure we were all ok. The old man that was holding onto Billy, got so scared that he was having chest pains and he unfastened his seatbelt. Billy asked about him and they told him he had a heart attack, but would be fine. Poor guy got so scared, it almost killed him. We had no cell service where we were, so we couldn't tell anyone we were ok, but Billy kept checking every few minutes in hopes he could make at least one call and that person could let everyone know we were alive.

We were given a free hotel by the airline to stay overnight and we would be leaving on another plane in the morning to finish our trip to Italy. I didn't want to get on another plane, ever. Billy said that was normal, but this doesn't happen all the time and we would be fine. The airline paid for our dinner and room and we ate and showered and went to relax in bed. Billy and I held each other all night and he comforted me. I slept pretty good considering what we went through and we got up and had breakfast, courtesy of the airline.

We were taken back to the airport and we boarded another plane that took us to Italy. I was petrified the whole time. It was only an hour and a half, but I was not comfortable at all and I wanted to get off. Billy and I got a drink in hopes it would help us relax. One didn't do it, so we ordered a few more. We were pretty tipsy when we got off the plane and we weren't the only ones, but it helped us both relax.

Billy was able to make a phone call to his parents and let them know we were ok and we were here and I made one to my parents to tell them the same. They were so relieved and said they saw it all on the news.

We got to our resort and just collapsed on the bed and fell asleep. We were both fucking drunk and we slept well into the afternoon. We got up and got ready to go out for dinner and I felt so much better after sleeping. We really needed to do that to relax our bodies.

We started our honeymoon in Rome and we went to La Terrazza. It was a Mediterranean rooftop restaurant and piano lounge with panoramic views. The views were better during the day, rather than night. We got there before dark, so we were able to see it both ways and enjoyed it more during daytime. It was gourmet dining and the views were so captivating. I found myself looking out the window, more than eating and drinking and Billy was doing the same. We both ordered food that we never had before. Billy got Goose Foie Gras and Peaches and I tasted it.

It wasn't what I expected. I thought it would be horrible and it was the opposite. Absolutely fantastic! There wasn't much of it. Italians eat in very small portions, unlike us Americans that stuff ourselves at each meal. I got Boeuf Braise, which is a braised beef. It was outstanding and so friggin tender, like nothing I ever had before. We both got the Tiramisu with a Twist for dessert and we had a cappuccino. After dinner, we went on a late night tour of the Colosseum to see it lit up and it was such a site to see. The pictures we took did not do it justice. You just have to see this in person to fully appreciate it.

Then we were on a search for some Gelato and finally found some. We walked the awesome streets of Rome, while eating our Gelato and did some people watching in the Piazzas. We went to the Catacombs at Night, where you walk deep underground and see some of the city's most incredible burial sites and you learn all about ancient Rome along the way. We enjoyed this one so much.

We headed back to the resort and we showered and Billy fueled the fire and we tucked ourselves into the luxurious bedding for some great sex on the first night of our honeymoon and so thankful to be alive.

We ordered breakfast from room service. They came with the cart and everything was so fancy. I answered the door and said, "Buongiorno." The man responded and I tipped him and said, "Grazie". He said, "Prego." We ordered a Cornetto which is an Italian croissant, made with Nutella or marmalade inside (oh yum) and we got cappuccino. This is the typical Italian Breakfast. Again, they eat very little at each meal, but they eat many meals throughout the day. The croissants are huge though. They didn't fill us up, but got us going for the day.

We were just going to wing it today and we were googling things to see in Rome.

We started the day by seeing the Pantheon. It is an iconic temple that was built 118 to 125 A.D. with a dome and Renaissance tombs. Next we went to Trevi Fountain, which is an Aqueduct-fed rococo fountain designed by Nicola Salvi and completed in 1762 with beautiful sculpted figures. Then we headed to the Roman Forum, which was a vast excavated area of Roman Temples square and government buildings, some dating back 2,000 years. Then we went to Piazza Navona which is an elegant square dating from the first century A.D. with a baroque fountain, street artists and bars. We went to St. Peter's Basilica, which is a Late Renaissance church by architects including Michelangelo. We were starving after seeing all these places and realized we had skipped lunch.

We went to Pane e Salame, which was near the Trevi Fountain. We ordered roast beef sandwiches with salsa tartara, (tartar sauce) pomodoro fresco (Cherry tomato sauce) and provolone and got a small cheese board. It was excellent.

Next we headed to Castel Sant'angelo. It is a circular, 2nd-Century castle that houses furniture and painting collections in Renaissance apartments. The Pope Quarters was very impressive. We went to the Spanish Steps and the steps were an irregular butterfly-shaped design and they were built in the 18th century at a French Diplomat's request. We got Gelato there and a guy offered me a rose. If you accept the rose they will ask for 2 Euro and Billy paid him. There were a lot of Brides there taking romantic pictures.

We went to the Sistine Chapel. It is the famous chapel in the Vatican Museums, best known for Michelangelo's 16th century painted ceiling. It was the most beautiful thing I have ever seen. We decided since it was almost time for dinner that we would do a Food Tour. You get to sample the best of Roman cuisine with a local guide. You get unlimited food and free flowing fine wine. We walked through the Prati neighborhood while sampling a variety of local delicacies. We were told that we would probably miss this if we were exploring on our own. We ate so much food, even though they were samples. Then we did a 3 in 1 cooking class Piazza Ancona. Fettuccine, Ravioli and Tiramisu.   After we made this food, we got to eat it and it was served with wine, limoncello and coffee. We had so much fun doing this together and it was well worth the money.

When we were done, we were so full from eating and tired from walking all day that we decided to call it a night and we went back to the resort and showered and he fueled the fire and fueled the fire and…and…we sunk into our plush silky comforter.

This was our last night in Rome and tomorrow we were headed for the Amalfi Coast. We got up and went to a place called Pasticceria Barberini and they make the most beautiful pastries. They are almost too pretty to eat, but as soon as you take a bite, you are glad you did. We got a few pastries to go and got a cappuccino and a cornetto with Nutella. This was our new favorite breakfast. It was also acceptable to eat cake for breakfast here. It seemed like everyone had cornetto's and cappuccino's on their table.

We went to the Amalfi Coast and checked out of our Rome Resort. Amalfi Coast is a stretch of coastline in southern Italy that overlooks the Tyrrhenian Sea and the Gulf of Salerno. The scenery here is just indescribable and it's a popular destination for people from all over the world. The water is a sapphire color and I was wondering if you could swim in it and the answer was yes. I told Billy that before we left, I wanted to at least stick my foot in, so I can say that I touched the water. He laughed and said we would find a place to go swimming. We found our hotel on the Amalfi Coast, called the Villa Piedmonte. It was so pretty inside, like something you would see on TV or in a magazine. It was absolutely gorgeous with every amenity you could think of. We were welcomed with a tray of food that was delivered to our door within minutes of arriving. We took the food out on the Terrazza, to eat and then got into our bathing suits and headed for Amalfi Beach. I wanted to swim here so bad. I don't know why, but I did. I wanted to be able to say that I swam at the

Amalfi Coast on Amalfi Beach. I enjoyed this day so much. We were at the beach for about 3 hours and then headed back for a shower and to change for lunch. Billy had the biggest smile on his face. He enjoyed it too. I looked at him and said, "We just swam on the Amalfi Coast". He picked me up and swung me around and said, "I am having such a good time here with you. I love you so much Em." I told him I loved him more.

We headed out to have some seafood at Marina Grande. It was a beachfront restaurant and had a great view over the sea. I got a cocktail called the Baba au rum. Oh My God. It was amazingly delicious. I got pasta with clams and Billy got Seafood Pasta and both were outstanding. I got the pastry Crumble Custard for dessert and Billy got the Lemon Delight cake. It sounds like a lot of food, but the portions are very small. I could have eaten about 4 of them. LOL. We Americans are pigs when it comes to eating. The pasta dishes were the size of an English muffin and the custard was a little bigger than a half dollar. Billy's cake was a little bigger, but my custard was like 2 tablespoons.

We had a scenic boat tour scheduled for the afternoon leaving from Sorrento and stopping in Positano and Amalfi to visit the towns, with time to swim, sip on Prosecco and taste snacks on board. This was my favorite part of our trip. We grabbed a sandwich and sat on the beach and relaxed. Then we hit the shops and more restaurants. We figured if we couldn't pig out in one restaurant, we could go to several. We really were pigs. We ate so much and we just couldn't get used to eating so many small meals. This way we got to try so many things. It was like a smorgasbord every night.

Next on our list was Venice. It was a city built on water and it's one of the most romantic cities in the world. It has no roads, just canals. It is known as the Floating City. It is lined with Renaissance and Gothic Palaces. We stayed at Corte Barozzi Venice Suites. We saw the Grand Casnasl, Saint Mark's Basilica, Doge's Palace, The Rialto Bridge and St. Mark's Square. We took a romantic singing Gondola Ride. I have always wanted to do this. We did a couple of different gondola rides. We walked across the Bridge of Sighs to the old prison.

The bridge was built in 1600 and made of white limestone and completely enclosed with latticed windows.

According to Venetian folk tales, those who kiss underneath this famous bridge are bound to find happiness and eternal love. We took a gondola ride and kissed under the bridge. We ate at a restaurant called Cantina Do Spade. It is a 600 year old wine bar and trattoria where the famous lover Casanova is said to have once entertained the women in his life. We also dined at Wisteria Ristorante.

We did as much as we could fit in and our honeymoon was coming to end. We had such a good time here and we vowed to come back someday.

I was scared to go back on the plane, although it was a different airline. Not that it makes a difference. I was really nervous, but Billy and I had a few drinks and fell asleep so we would be more comfortable. We made it home fine and I was glad when my feet hit the ground in the airport. I think Billy was happy to be home too. He never said it, but I think I saw him sigh when his feet hit the ground. We spent 10 days in Italy and had the best time ever. We texted our families to let them know we were home safe and we still had a few days before we went back to work. We unpacked and did laundry and we went grocery shopping. We separated all our gifts for everyone and put them all in gift bags. We went swimming and hit the hot tub and Billy put some burgers on the BBQ. I made some macaroni salad and we bought corn on the cob when we went shopping, so I boiled that up and we had a nice dinner outside on the deck.

16

NEW ADDITIONS

We cleaned up the dishes and went for a walk around the neighborhood and said hi to a few neighbors.

We were almost home and Billy stopped walking and said, "Sshhhh, Listen." I stopped and listened and we heard what sounded like a baby crying. We kept hearing it and Billy started walking toward a bush. He looked in the bush and then looked at me and smiled. "Come here." I went over and peeked in. "It's a kitten?" He said, "It's not a normal kitten, it's a baby bobcat." He started looking around to make sure the mother was no where to be found. He said, "If she is around, she will attack us." We backed away from the bush and just stood there for about 15 minutes.

The baby kept crying and no mom was in site. Billy said it looked very, very young and maybe the mom left him there. He said, "He is about 4-5 weeks. Maybe younger because they are big cats and the kittens look older than a regular kitten." I looked at him and said, "Are we just gonna leave him there Billy?" He looked at me and smiled, "I don't know. What should we do? Do you want to take him home?" We would have to get a box big enough for him and put him in the garage and get him food and stuff. This is a big responsibility babe." I said, "Maybe we could take him to a vet and they can tell us what to do or maybe they would take him? I don't want to leave him here. He is just a baby."

Billy checked the bushes all around to make sure there were no other babies and no mother. He picked up the baby and cuddled him and then handed him to me. My heart melted when I touched him. He snuggled into me and I knew I didn't want to give him up, but I didn't say anything. I don't think I had to because Billy was smiling at me. I said, "Do people keep bob cats Billy?" He said, "Yeah, they do, if you get them young enough, you train them to be like a regular kitten."   I said, "Let's take him to a vet and find out what's involved in taking care of him. I never had a pet before." He agreed that it was a smart idea.

We took him to Blue Pearl Pet Hospital. They were open 24 hours because they were an emergency veterinary hospital. People were staring at us when we walked in and coming up to us and petting him. He was such a beautiful animal. There weren't too many people in there so we didn't have to wait long.

The vet said the baby was healthy and we probably should have left him there. He said we could put him back, but the mother might reject him, or he could contact an experienced bobcat rehabber. He told us that we do not want to bring the cat inside our house or keep him as a pet. He explained that he will never be fully domesticated and might be dangerous down the road. He said he would take the baby and take care of it until he contacted the rehabber. I looked at Billy and said, "Should we put him back where we found him?" The vet said that because we touched him, he had our scent on him, so the mother might reject him now. We handed him over to the vet and he said he would take care of him for the time being. He said we could call to get updates on him. We left and I felt sad. "We should have left him alone, but then what if the mother never came back for him? He would have died there or got hit by a car. It's just not fair." Billy took my hand and said, "I know babe, but he will be in good hands now and at least we will know that he will be taken care of."

We went home, showered and got into bed for some… and TV. We watched a couple of shows and fell asleep. When I woke up, Billy was gone. I walked downstairs calling him. "Billy?, Billy?" I found a note on the counter in the kitchen. "Good Morning beautiful. We forgot to buy coffee pods. I will be back soon. Love Billy XOXO". He was gone for a long time and I was getting worried. I was going to wait for 10 more minutes and then text him. 5 minutes went by and he drove into the driveway and got out of the car with a box and 2 big bags.

I opened the door for him and he walked in with a huge smile on his face. "I got the coffee pods. I can't believe we forgot them. And I picked up something else." I said, "What did you get?" He put the box on the counter and said, "Open it." I opened the box and it was a

Tabby Kitten and it looked just like the bob cat we found, but a lot smaller. He had black and gray stripes and blue eyes. He was so tiny. "Omg, Billy, he is so friggin cute. Where did you find him?" He said, "I saw him last night at the vet and he was up for adoption, so I went back to get him. What do you think? Do you want to keep him? Are you ready for a pet?" I picked him up and snuggled him and started crying. "Yes, I want to keep him. OH God, I love you Billy. Look how cute he is."

He opened the bags up and he had a litter box, litter, kitten dry food and wet food and a brush and bowls and the vet gave him vitamins and some other stuff. I couldn't put this baby down.   I just cuddled him and he let me. I said, "We need a name, but I want it to be a cute name and not one that everyone uses. It has to be special. Billy said, "How bout Halo or Suki?" He paused and said, "Ramsey?, Nugget? OH, I know, How bout Buko?" "Yes, Buko, I love it. That is his name." Billy was making coffee as we were talking. I was still holding the kitten. Billy looked at me and said, "I felt bad because we had to leave the bob cat at the vet and I saw

how sad you were. It's time for us to have a
pet or two. I was going to get another one so
they would have company, but I figured I
better only bring home one, just in case you
didn't want it." I smiled at him and said, "I
think we should go get another one. I love him
already and he needs company. Billy set up
the litter box in the small bath down the hall
and we put him in it and let him walk around.
We set up the dishes in the kitchen and put dry
food in it. I told him he forgot a bed for him.
He smiled and said, "Let's go, Grab Buko and
we will take him with us and go get him a
brother or sister and a couple of beds." I was
so happy because these were going to be my
very first pets. I hope I will be a good kitty
mom. I always had doubts about myself
caring for someone or something. I don't
know why, but I did. We went back to the vet
and he smiled at us and thought we were
bringing the kitten back. Billy said, "No, we
came back to get another one. Did you say
this guy had a brother or sister?" The vet
laughed and said, "They are addicting and yes,
he has a brother. Let me go get him."

He came back with another kitten that looked exactly like Buko, except he had black hair on the tips of his ears. He was adorable. Billy snatched him up and asked the vet for a box. Billy told him we were off to the pet store for a carrier and a couple of beds and toys. Billy gave the vet a $100 donation and thanked him for helping us and we got to see the Bob cat kitten and he was doing fine. The kittens had all their shots for 8 weeks, so they were all set. We got in the car and Billy said, "We are now parents Em." I looked at him and said, "I hope I will be a good parent." He said, "Of course you will." I looked at him and said, "I have a name for your kitty." He looked at me and said, "Oh, this one is mine? What do you have in mind?" I said, "Barley. Barley and Buko.

What do you think?" He smiled at me and said, "I love it. It's Perfect." We went to the pet store and got a carrier for the kitties and we put them in right away and put them in the carriage and drove them around the store while we shopped for everything else we needed. We kind of went overboard with toys, a cat tree and blankets and stuff, but these were our kids, our babies and we wanted to spoil them. We took everything to the register and the cashier fell in love with the kitties in the crate and said, "This is a first. I am ringing out a crate full of kitties."

We took them home and got them settled in and showed them both the litter boxes (we had to get another one). They both went off wondering and checking out the house and we kept an eye on them and then we kept them in a zippered tent at night time with their beds, food, water and a litter box. We didn't want them to get into anything while we were sleeping. We kept the tent in our bedroom so they wouldn't be alone. It worked out great and they slept together and they were quiet all night long.

Billy fueled the fire while we were watching TV and we were getting really hot and he was getting into it. We transferred to the bedroom and the fire was lit. God how I loved this man. He was sweet, caring, loving, sensitive, kind, confident, supportive, romantic, appreciative, a good listener and communicator and he had a sense of humor. What more could I ask for? He had it all and he was mine.

I couldn't believe he brought me a kitten. It made me so friggin happy. He said he felt bad because we had to leave the bob cat kitten at the vet and he knew I wanted it. I did want it and I think he wanted it too. As soon as I cuddled with him, I fell in love. When he brought me Buko, I fell in love with him too. Maybe I was just meant to be an animal mom. And now we had Barley and Buko and they were all cuddled up together in their bed after having a snack, some water and using the litter box. We spent the whole next day with kittens in our laps and petting and talking to them and playing with them. I was so in love with them already and so was Billy. Billy took a selfie of both of us holding the kittens and sent the picture in a group text that said, "Welcome to our family Barley and Buko." And of course, everyone was commenting on how cute they were. No one on either side of our families had a pet. We were the first to have them.

Everyone was asking us questions about them and Billy told everyone it all started because we found a bob cat kitten. He only had one picture of the bob cat kitten and I was holding him. He told everyone that after we had to leave the bob cat kitten with the vet, we were sad, so we adopted one and then the other one. He said, "Now our family is complete." Everyone wished us good luck with them and said they couldn't wait to meet them.

We had a few more days off before returning to work and we spent the whole time with our new kittens. We were addicted to them and so in love. They were starting to get used to the house and they were running around and playing with each other. We decided that when we went to work, we would close them up in one room so they wouldn't get into trouble or be in any danger and they would still be able to run around and play. But for the time being, we were home and we let them go wherever they wanted and get used to the house.

They scouted around and poked their little noses into everything. They were so little and they hopped like little bunnies. They had tiny little meows that sounded like squeaks. God they were so friggin cute. They were cuddlers and they stayed in our laps to take their naps and at night, they got used to going in their little zippered up pen for the night. We had so much fun with them every single day. I really didn't want to go back to work and leave them. Billy admitted that he loved being around them and he didn't want to go back either. He laughed and said, "Maybe we can take them to work and I will leave them in my office." I laughed and said, "I don't think that will go over too well and I am sure there is at least one person that is allergic to cats in the office."

We went grocery shopping the following day and left the kittens in their room and closed the door. We checked to make sure there was nothing they could get into and left. They were fine and they were both sleeping when we got home. We let them out and they were romping around while we were putting the groceries away. All of a sudden we heard one of them screaming. We both freaked out. "Where is he? Where is he?" Apparently, Billy opened up the pantry and put something in and left the door open to get something else that belonged in there and then shut the door. Buko got locked into the pantry. Billy opened the door and he was just sitting their screaming. He picked him up and cuddled him and said, "Maybe you will learn not to go in there now. Poor baby. So scared." He held him for a while, and continued to put groceries away, and then put him down and he was fine. I started laughing and said, "This will not be the first time they freak us out. The vet also told me to watch out for the plastic shopping bags and not to let them play in them because they can suffocate and also can get caught in the handle and twist it around their neck and choke, so don't leave any around, even if they have stuff in them." Billy was listening intently and said, "Wow, ok, yeah that sounds dangerous. For that matter, anything with a handle." I shook my head yes.

Our last few days were spent with our new babies. We spent every waking moment with them. We ate with them in our laps and played with them and spoiled them rotten.

17

GIFTS AND TREATS

We went to work on Monday and everyone welcomed us back and we were showing them tons of pictures and telling them our tales of romantic adventures. We had our monthly meeting in the large conference room and Billy told everyone that we had a family now and everyone got quiet.

He took out his phone and passed it around with the selfie that we took with Buko and Barley. He told everyone the story of our walk and how we found a baby bob cat kitten and then how he felt bad when we left him at the vet and adopted Buko and how we went back for Barley. He showed everyone the picture of the bob cat kitten. Everyone was excited for us and thought our new babies were so cute. Attorney Kaufman held the phone for quite a while and then said, "They are really beautiful animals. I am thinking of getting one." Billy said, "You have to get two so they have company." Kaufman shook his head and said,

"Yup, gonna do it." And he handed the phone back to Billy.

We all went back to work and I was trying to catch up on certain things. Evelyn covered for me while I was out and she did a lot of my work and I appreciated her so much. I asked her to come into my office and I gave her the gift I bought her in Italy and she loved it. I bought her a cream colored sweatshirt that said Venice Italy and had an embroidered canal with a gondola underneath and underneath it, it said, Travel in Italia.

I bought my other paralegals embroidered sweatshirts that said Amalfi Italia in different colors. Billy bought gifts for Attorney Kaufman and for his secretary and he bought little magnets for all the other secretaries in the whole office. For all the other attorneys, he bought bottles of wine (which we had shipped to us) and he bought a huge box, called Tastes from Italy and it had all kinds of snacks and candy and he put it on the table in the kitchen for everyone to enjoy.

It was really hard for me to get back into the groove after our awesome vacation and our new babies that were home alone. Billy peeked into the office just before lunch and said, "Wanna take a ride home to check on our kids?" I jumped up and grabbed my purse and said, "You know I do." We took an extended lunch because it took awhile to get home and back, not to mention eating our lunch and loving on the babies. We put the extra time on our time sheets so we were good. The babies were fine. They were playing on their cat tree and there were toys everywhere in their room. They spilled their dry food all over the place, so we cleaned it up and gave them some more.

They didn't get into anything in there because we cleaned it all out before we put them in there. It was a hardwood floor, so there were no rugs to scratch. We had a couple of scratch pads in there and we noticed that they used them. We put a couple of little rugs in there under the litter boxes and the scratchers. There were only cat things in the room. A cat tree, litter boxes, the rugs, toys, food and water. We headed back to work and Billy was fueling the fire before he started the car. "I miss being with you all day and loving on you whenever I wanted to. Work sucks." He laughed and I laughed and said, "Yes it does. I was having a hard time getting back into it. I didn't do very much yet today. We had the meeting this morning and then I did a few things and it was lunchtime. Oh, and I miss you loving on me all day too." I fueled the fire.

We got back to work, and of course, we had to get going and get back into working. The day went by fast because there was a lot of work to catch up on and we went home. Billy didn't waste anytime fueling the fire when he got into the car with me. He said, "Let's go out for dinner or we can order, pick it up and take it home to eat. Whatever you want to do." I said, "Doesn't matter to me. You decide." He smiled and said, "Ok, let's go out to eat." We went to a steak house call Bin 54 Steak and Cellar. I got the Blackened Chili Lime Shrimp and Billy got the Lobster Gnocchi. Both were excellent and we enjoyed every bite. We walked back to the car and he fueled my fire the whole way.

The first thing we did was open the door to see our babies. They were both sleeping together in one bed and all curled up. They were definitely not watch cats because they didn't even flinch when we opened the door. Billy and I went to change and shower and we left the door open for them. We got out and they were still sleeping. We snuggled into the couch to watch some TV and Billy got some ice cream for the both of us. All of a sudden, we heard meows coming from the other room and we called them to us. "BARLEY, BUKO, COME ON BABIES". They both came running and making little meows. They missed us so much. They climbed up on the couch and into our laps and wanted to see what we were eating. I put some on my finger and Billy did the same and we let them taste the ice cream. It was vanilla, so it would be ok. I told Billy that they couldn't have anything chocolate and he said he was aware of that. We cuddled with each other and our kitties and a couple hours later, we headed for the bedroom and put the kitties in their zippered tent and off to sleep they went.

Our families got to meet them down the road. My mom and dad came down to visit and Barley and Buko were still little. I think they were about 6 months. They instantly fell in love with them and decided to get a couple kittens when they went home. My brother Jesse wanted a couple too. Jack did not come with Izzy because they had the baby and didn't want to travel with her yet. My mom sent pictures of their babies. They were brother and sister and they named them Nugget and Nala. Billy gave Nugget his name and my mom picked Nala.

Billy's parents came to visit before my parents did because they were in Raleigh and only 40 minutes away. His mother said she wanted a kitten and his father said no. He didn't want a pet and she said, "Then move out, because I am getting a kitten when I get home." He looked at her shocked and said, "I am not going anywhere and you are not getting a kitten." Billy and I looked at each other and left the room and we took our kittens with us. They argued for about 15 minutes and we just listened from the other room. It got quiet, so we came back out into the living room and Billy said, "So, what's the verdict?" His father laughed and said, "She won. We are getting a kitten." He smiled at his father and said,

"Good man." His mother was all smiles. I said, "We didn't mean to start a fight, but they really are awesome and so much company." I was holding Buko and said, "Look how cute." I brought him up to his dad and he pet him. "I know, I know, Ok." I laughed at him and said, "You won't be sorry at all, but make sure you get two of them so they have company. You will have one and Anna will have one." He looked at me and said, "Two? I didn't agree on two." I said, "You really should agree on two or you will be sorry you didn't. You need to get two the same age, so they grow up together and they will love each other. Preferably, 2 males because males are much more affectionate." Anna was looking at me and then Dan. I said, "Well? What do you say to two?" He smiled at me and then at Anna and said, "Ok two, but no more than that and no other animals." She hugged me and then Dan and said thank you to both of us. And so it was. They got two kittens that were 8 weeks old and Billy and I helped them get what they needed at the pet store and Dan was so happy and he was hugging them. They named their kittens, Ruger and Ramsey. Billy named Ramsey and his dad named Ruger. I looked at Billy and said, "See what we started?" He fueled my fire and continued all night long. Thank God tomorrow was Sunday.

18

MEET NICK

Sunday morning we got up and Billy made breakfast and we went out on the enclosed porch to eat it. The weather was perfect out there and he set everything up so nice. He even picked some flowers from out back and put them in a vase on the table. There was only one problem. There was a bumble bee in the flowers, but he tried. We were running around trying to get away from it and we ended up laughing while we were trying to swat it. Buko and Barley were trying to get it and they were jumping up and down and swatting. If anyone was watching us, they would have thought we were all crazy. And wouldn't you know, someone was watching us.

Our neighbor (who we have never met) was out in his enclosed porch and he was laughing. Billy laughed and told him it was a bee. Billy ended up asking him to come over for a cup of coffee and he accepted. He came to the screen door and Billy opened it up for him and shook his hand and introduced himself and me and he came and shook my hand. He was an older gentleman about 60, I think. I wasn't sure and Billy thought he was about 50, so I could be wrong. His name was Nick. He seemed nice and told us that his wife died last year and he was thinking about selling his house because it was big and he was the only one living there and he said he and his wife never had kids. Billy picked up Buko and he said, "These guys are our kids." Billy told him to have a seat and he would go get him a cup of coffee. He struck up a conversation about the cats with me and told me that they were beautiful and that he never got a pet. I told him and kinda of laughed, that he should get a cat and told him how we got ours and then Billy's parents and my parents got them because we did. He laughed and said, "They are so adorable." I had Barley in my lap and Buko was in Billy's chair. He asked their names and I told him. I said, "They are so much company and so lovable. Of course, we spoiled them rotten." He asked where we got them and I told him. Billy came in with the coffee and put it in front of him. He added sugar and creamer and sipped it and thanked Billy. Billy said, "Is my wife talking you into getting a kitten?" He was chuckling. Nick laughed and said, "Yes, but she didn't really have to do much. I never thought about getting a pet for company, but these guys are so lovable and I think I might just do it. I think it might be good for me. I am really missing my wife." Billy touched his hand and said, "I am so sorry. If you need anything, let us know." Nick thanked him. Billy asked if he had breakfast and told him we had plenty. Nick said, "It sure looks good. I would love some." Billy gave him a paper plate and he dug into the scrambled eggs and sausage and toast and we all ate together. He was so thankful just for the company.

I felt bad for him and told him we were having Chicken Parmesan with spaghetti for supper and asked if he would like join us. His face lit up and said, "That would be wonderful. Thank you so much. What time should I come? Can I bring something?" I told him we were eating around 6 and he should just bring himself. He thanked us for the breakfast and left with a big smile on his face. He petted the cats before he left.

The rest of the day was quiet. I prepared supper with Billy's help and we played a couple games of cards out on the deck. We went in the hot tub for a while and then came in to rest before dinner. We laid down on the bed in our sweats and he lit the fire and got it going really good. It was rip roaring hot and we really got into it. We laid there for a while and then got up to put the chicken parmesan in the oven and Billy put the pot of water on for the spaghetti. We both put a nice salad together and we set the dining room table and Billy got a bottle of wine from the rack. He said, "It was nice that you invited him for dinner. It sounds like he is really lonely and starved for company." I told him, "I just followed your footsteps, seeing as you invited him for breakfast. He was so happy."

Our front doorbell rang and it was Nick. He was carrying a bottle of wine, flowers and a bakery box and he looked like he was about to drop it all. Billy grabbed the wine and flowers and he came walking in with the biggest smile on his face. He handed me the box and said, "I brought dessert. I never go anywhere, unless I bring something." He took the flowers from Billy and handed them to me and said, "These are for you honey. Thank you for being so kind and Billy, the wine is for you for being kind. Thank you, Thank you." Billy showed him to the dining room and we had the salad out on the table with a few salad dressings, so he could take his pick. The smile never left his face. He was a such a jolly man and very sweet. Billy and I came in with the Tray of Chicken Parmesan and a Bowl of Spaghetti and his whole face lit up. "Is this homemade?" I smiled and said, "Yes, Nick, Billy and I made it this afternoon. I hope you enjoy it." He was licking his chops and couldn't wait to dig in. Billy helped him get the spaghetti and said, "Say when". I served him a large piece of chicken and topped everything off with some more sauce and asked if he wanted some grated cheese and of course his answer was YES please. Billy started asking him questions about his family and he told us that he had no family at all. He said, "I had a brother but he died of a heart attack two years ago and then last year my wife died. She was an only child. My parents of course, have passed away." Billy asked him how old he was and he shocked both of us by saying "75". I said, "OMG Nick, I thought you were like 60 and Billy said "50".   He smiled and said, "Oh Thank you. At my age, that is a big compliment." Billy asked him if he had any friends and he put his head down and said, "Well all my friends died already, so I am completely alone and now I have you wonderful people as friends and I cherish you both." I almost started crying. That is so very sad. How can you lose everyone you ever knew? I guess it really happens to people and I hope it never happens to me. Billy touched his shoulder and said, "It's nice to have you as a friend too, Nick."

We had some more conversation as I cleared the dishes. I told Billy to just stay and talk and I would clean up, but Nick got up to help so Billy did too. Nick picked up his dish and brought it to the kitchen. Billy brought in all the dressings and salad and had the table completely cleared off by the time Nick got back to the table. Billy made a pot of coffee and brought it in to the dining room and I got the box out that Nick brought and opened it up. Wow… he brought an assortment of pastries. Chocolate Eclairs, Cannoli's, Cookies, Rum Pastries and a few other things. I put them all on the platter and brought it in. "Thank you for the pastries, Nick. They look yummy." He smiled and said, "Your welcome. I didn't know what you guys like, so I got an assortment." Billy said, "The problem is that we like all of them." Billy was laughing and Nick laughed with him. Billy poured everyone's coffee. I was still full from dinner and said, "If you guys want to wait before eating dessert, we can. I know I am too full." Nick agreed that he was too full."

We had a nice evening and had our dessert and then Nick went home and we showered and got ready for work the next day.

Our work week was busy and went by pretty fast and the weekend was here again. Nick would peek over his fence and say hi when we were outside. Billy asked him to come over for coffee a couple times during the week and he happily accepted. It was a Friday night and Billy and I had gone out for supper and when we got home we noticed a car in Nick's driveway. Billy texted him to make sure he was ok, because he told us that no one ever came to his house and he had no family or friends. Nick answered the text and said he was fine. He told Billy that it was his lawyer and that he was making some changes to his will. Billy said, "Ok, I wasn't trying to be nosey. I just wanted to make sure you were ok." Nick said, "Thank you for checking on me. I really appreciate that."

We went inside and went out on the patio to have a cup of coffee. We played a few card games while we were sitting there. We had a deck of cards on the table that stayed there. We liked to play 5 or 7 card stud and some other poker games. Billy loved to play cards and got me interested in them and he taught me how to play the games.

Nick texted Billy and asked if we had a safe and Billy told him we did. He said, "Can I give you something to put in your safe for me. I hate to ask, but it's kind of important and I don't have one. Do you mind?" Billy told him he didn't mind at all and to bring over. We kind of figured it was his Will because his lawyer was at the house. He came over with a little envelope and handed it to Billy. He said, "Billy, this is my Last Will and Testament and I have no one else to hold it for me. I hope you don't mind, but I named you as my Executor. Is that ok?" Billy was stunned. "Really Nick? Wow, I am honored and I will go put it in the safe right now. I will be right back." Billy never opened the Will and put it on a separate shelf in our safe and came back. Nick was smiling at us and we offered him some coffee and a piece of cake, that I had made during the week. Nick never said no to coffee and cake.

He never talked about his Will or his lawyer. He said he went to the grocery store earlier today and got a few things to eat. He told us that he got pre-cooked food so he just had to heat it up. "At my age, it would be stupid to buy stuff to cook with, because it's just me. My wife used to do all the cooking but now she is gone. God how I miss her." He sipped his coffee and ate his cake and Billy was talking about the cats and he had one in his lap and I had one in my lap. They usually did that every night when we were sitting out there. They loved the petting and attention and they were very lovable animals and we loved them with all our hearts. Most people talk about their kids, but we talked about our cats.

Nick went home and Billy and I locked up and went to take a shower and fuel the fire. We sank into our bed and watched TV until we fell asleep.

The next morning, we planned on going out for breakfast and as we were walking out of the house, Billy said, "Wanna invite Nick?" I shook my head yes and we walked back into the house. Billy sent him a text and asked him and he responded that he would love to. We gave him a few minutes to get ready and then walked out the front door and met him in the driveway. We went to Breakaway Cafe and we all had a really nice breakfast together. Nick was so happy that we invited him. Billy and I took a liking to him. It was hard <u>not</u> to like him and he had nobody and we felt sorry for him.

We went home and Nick thanked us for breakfast and went home. Billy and I talked about him that afternoon. It felt like he was our adopted grandpa and it felt really good to make him happy.

We visited Billy's parents that afternoon and we told them the story about Nick and how sad his situation was. Anna kept looking at me and finally I said, "What's up Anna? Is there something wrong?" She said, "Oh no, why?" I said, "I don't know, you keep staring at me, so I was just wondering if there was something wrong." Billy and his Dad were listening from the living room and Liz was there visiting as well. Anna said, "I just can't believe that I got you all wrong. You are a sweet girl Emily, for taking Nick under your wing. I love that both of you did that. That's all." I smiled at her and said, "Ok, Yes, he is kind of our adopted grandpa of sorts. It just feels good to make him smile and be happy. He is growing on us." We had a nice visit and we went home.

As usual, we went outside in the patio for our coffee. Billy peeked over to see if Nick was outside, but he wasn't. We had our coffee and cleaned up and got comfy in bed. Sunday morning, we decided to stay in for the day and make breakfast and dinner at home. We both cooked breakfast and planned some ravioli, salad and garlic bread for dinner. It would be nice and easy and quick too. We didn't hear anything from Nick on Sunday and we figured he was probably watching football as he normally did. He said he didn't want to overdo his visits and we told him he wasn't, but he said we wouldn't see him everyday.

Monday we went back to work and decided to go out for dinner that night. We got home and fed our kitties and settled in for the night.

Billy looked at me funny and said, "I just got a bad feeling." I looked at him and said, "What babe?" He looked like he was going to cry and his eyebrows were narrowed down. I went up to him and touched his face. "What's wrong babe? Are you ok?" He said, "I am ok, but I think something happened to Nick. I don't know why, but I got this bad feeling. I am going next door to check on him." He was barefoot and had his sweatpants and sweatshirt on and he walked over to his house and knocked on the door. I stood on our front porch. He kept knocking and calling him. "NICK NICK, NICK". There was no answer and he did not come to the door. Billy walked around back and his slider door was unlocked. He knocked at it and no answer, so he slid it open and called him again. "NICK?" He walked into the living room and the TV was on with a football game on and Nick was sitting in his recliner. Billy checked him and he was cold. He called 9-1-1. He wasn't breathing and Billy got so upset he was crying. I walked over and he told me not to come in. "He's dead babe." He was crying and I came in anyway. I hugged him and rubbed his back and started crying too. The ambulance came and Billy opened the front door and he told them he wasn't breathing and that he had passed. We were both still crying. The firemen asked us if we were his relatives and we told them we were neighbors and that he had no one and we were just checking on him. Billy told him that we had his Last Will in our safe and that he gave it to us last week to hold onto. Billy said, "I am the Executor of his Will, but he had no one, so we kind of looked after him." Billy gave him his cell number to contact us for funeral arrangements and that he had to go check out the Will to see what it said.

They took him away and Billy found his house key and we took it and made sure everything was locked up and we walked home.

19

LAST WILL AND TESTAMENT

He went to the safe and pulled out the Will. Nick did not want a funeral, but he wanted to be cremated and wanted his ashes spread out on Sunset Beach. Billy was reading and reading and then he looked at me and smiled with tears coming out of his eyes. "He left everything to us babe. We were all he had and he left it all to us." I was shocked. "What? Oh My God." Billy said, "He wants us to go through his house and take what we want and then sell it and keep the profit and it is paid for." He kept reading. "Holy Fucking Shit Em. This guy was loaded. He could have had anything he wanted, but all he wanted was company and he couldn't buy that." He started sobbing again. "He left us everything Em. Everything…He has CD's, Money Market accounts, Savings Accounts, Checking Accounts and a Retirement Account." He kept reading and then said, "He has a safe in his living room floor underneath the rug in front of the couch. Whatever is in there belongs to us." I just sat there saying, "Oh My God."

Billy looked at me and he said, "I wasn't nice to him because I expected something in return. I loved that old man like he was my Grandpa." He was sobbing again and I sobbed with him. I said, "I feel the same way babe." He said, "He died doing what he loved. Watching Football."   Billy started second guessing himself and said, "I wonder if he died on Saturday night, because he wasn't around all day on Sunday and his body was cold? I should have checked on him earlier and I probably could have helped him." I rubbed his back and said, "It was just his time babe. No matter when you checked on him, it was just his time." He shook his head and he knew I was right. I said, "We made him happy the last few weeks of his life. We gave him what he needed. He needed Company and friendship and we gave that to him. We invited him for coffee, cake and dinner and out for breakfast and that made him happy. That is what he needed and now he is back with his wife." Billy smiled at me and said, "You always make me feel better, no matter what the situation is."

We followed Nick's wishes and had him cremated and we rented a boat and spread his ashes out at the beach as he requested. We went through his house and it turns out his wife had a collection of Ancient ceramics from the Italian renaissance and she had a collection of Imperial Chinese porcelain cups. They were worth thousands of dollars. They were all packed up in the basement. We had to go through every single box to make sure we weren't throwing expensive stuff away. The safe in the living room floor had tons of jewelry that belonged to his wife. There were ruby bracelets and necklaces and rings and diamonds galore. We were guessing that she was born in July because of all the ruby stones. There were expensive watches in there that belonged to Nick and his wife. There were tons of gold chains and bracelets of all kinds and all designs. There were a lot of coins in an envelope in the safe as well and we had to have them appraised, along with the jewelry. We had our work cut out for us. It took us months to go through the house.

There were 5 bedrooms of stuff in every closet and every crevice. The basement was full of sealed boxes and not all of them were labeled.

I have to say that the house was neat and organized, but it was not clean at all. I never thought it would be because poor Nick couldn't do it. There was so much dust and so many cobwebs and it looked like it hadn't been cleaned in decades. We cleaned everything out of the house and called in a junk place to come and get everything else.

We had the house professionally cleaned and put it on the market. It took us 6 months to clean out the house because there was so much stuff. We stacked all the boxes of stuff that we had to go through in our garage. Billy and I claimed all the money he left. The CD's were all put in our names, but we left them there in the bank until they matured. They still had another 6 months. There were 6 CD's and each one was for $50,000, so that was $300,000. He had $10,000 in his checking account. He had 3 savings accounts in 3 different banks and they all had $250,000 in them, because I guess it wasn't insured above that amount. The 3 Money Market Accounts had $150,000 in each one in separate banks.

We had no idea what Nick did for a living, but we did keep a couple boxes of personal things so we could find out some information on Nick and his wife. We sold the house and got $800,200 for it. We didn't counter with the buyers at all. We put it up for $805,000. They put in an offer and we accepted it. We ended up paying off our house in full and we both bought a new car. We donated $10,000 to the shelter down the street. We had gone there to adopt Anna and Dan's kittens and they really needed the donation and they were so appreciative. I always donated food to them after visiting and they were grateful for it.

20

BOXES GALORE

Billy wanted me to stay home, but I argued with him. "What am I going to do if I stay home? I will be bored stiff." He laughed and said, "You can start by going through all those boxes we have in our garage. I am dying to know what Nick did for a living." I told him we could both stay home and do that and he said, "Not right now, but I am thinking about it and it won't be long." I said, "Ok, well when you do it, I will too." He laughed at me. "Ok. Deal."

No one at work knew what happened to us with our neighbor Nick and I told Billy he should have a conference about Team Players and use Nick as an example of how a smile or doing something to help, makes people happy, but he didn't want to do that. He did, however, have a meeting about Team Players and then told our story about Nick and half the conference room was in tears. He didn't tell them how much money we came into, but he did tell them that he left us everything he had. He also told everyone that we were thinking of leaving the firm, but it wouldn't be right away. Everyone got very quiet and they couldn't believe it.

We invited my parents and brothers and family to come down for a week and we both took a couple weeks off. We also invited his parents and sisters and family, to come for a day and we had a huge catered dinner together and we broke the news about Nick. Anna and Dan knew he died because we told them right away. My mom and dad knew about what we did for him and they were so proud that we did that for him. Neither of our parents knew that he left us everything and they couldn't believe it. We didn't share how much he left us, but they knew we made a lot money on the house. We told them that we paid off our house and bought new cars and that we were well off and thinking about quitting our jobs. Anna was shocked and had her mouth open and said, "He left you that much hon?" Billy said, "Yes mom. He left us everything he had. It was a lot and all because we were nice to him and gave him what he needed. Company and friendship!! That is all he wanted. I can't tell you how proud I am of myself. He was like a

grandpa to us and he made us love him."
They stayed the day and went home and my
parents stayed for the week and Nick was the
major conversation almost all week. We even
toasted him a few times, once with coffee.

Billy was still visibly upset over his death and
he told me that he was just getting to know
him and he left. "I thought I would have him
around for a while. He was such a nice man."

We both got to see my little niece who was
almost 2 years old now. Cutest niece EVER!!
Jack and Izzy were good parents and Jack
was the best Daddy. It was good to see my
brothers and my mom and dad again. I
missed them and we hadn't seen them in a
long time. Billy and I were in bed talking one
night and he said, "We should buy a place in
Connecticut and we can live there part of the
year, so you get some time with your parents
and your family. I would love to live near the
beach. Actually, I would love to live on the
beach in a cottage or something like that.
What do you think of that?" I looked at him
and said, "Really? You want to live in a
cottage on the beach in Connecticut?" He

shook his head yes. I said, "I am IN. Yes, let's do it. But first, we need to go through all those boxes of Nick's and find out his story and we need to quit our jobs and take care of things here first." He shook his head and said, "Absolutely."

My parents left to go home and we all had a nice visit together. My mom and I had a lot of one on one's while she was there. I took her to lunch and we went for manicures and pedicures together. I took her out for ice cream and we went clothes shopping. Billy entertained while we were gone and he was really good at it. I invited my sister-in-laws to come with us, but they knew my mom wanted that time with me, so they stayed home.

They left on a Friday afternoon and Billy went out to the garage and brought in a box and said, "No time like the present. Let's see what Nick had his hands into." He opened the box and started rifling through papers. He was skimming them and I told him, if he skimmed, he wasn't going to find out anything. The first paper on top was the sale of a property (a condo) on a ski resort in Colorado. He owned property on a ski resort that was bringing in oodles of money every month, but he sold it and got $500,000. The second paper was the sale of an Airbnb in New Hampshire. It had 3 bedrooms and 1 bath and he bought it for $300,000 and every month he got rental income of $4,500.00. He sold it for $400,000.

He made several investments and he also played the stock market. His wife's name was Edith and he called her Eddie, according to the papers and letters we found. She belonged to Collectors Collections and she owned a lot of very expensive things, like porcelain ware and ancient dishes and coins. She sold some before she passed away and the receipt was in the box as well. She made $765,000 for what she sold. Holy Shit. I took pictures of all the receipts. She had some kind of blog on the internet, and she was selling other things that were handmade. There were pictures of earrings, bracelets and necklaces and she made quite a bit of money doing that. So most of the money came from investment properties and ancient china.

Underneath all those papers was a big brown envelope with a tie closure. I opened it and saw casino coins (poker chips or gaming tokens) The whole envelope was full of them. I took one out and looked at it. It was a $1,000 chip and then I poured some more out of the envelope and they were all for $1,000. Billy and I looked at each other and just said, "Holy Shit." Under that envelope was another one that said, "Bronco Billy's Casino." Billy opened it up laughing and said, "My name is on it, so I am opening this one." We were both laughing, but the laughing stopped when he dumped out the envelope. It was cash, all cash in $1,000 bills. The envelope was full of them. Billy said, "What the fuck? This guy really gambled. Why is the money in a box in an envelope though?" I said, "Maybe Eddie didn't know he was gambling and he was hiding it?"

Billy took the envelopes with the money and chips and ran it off to the safe. When he came back, I was deep into another envelope from a casino in California called Coyote Valley

Casino. It was full of chips and money. "Oh My God Billy. Look at this shit." His eyes were bulging out of his head. He took the envelope and went back to the safe.

When he got back I was still going through the box and there were smaller brown envelopes towards the bottom with peoples names on them. One was addressed to his brother, but never mailed. "This is the brother that passed away so maybe he didn't mail it because he had passed before he sent it." Billy opened it and there was $100,000 in it. "Jesus Mary." We took the other brown envelopes out of the box. There were 6, with peoples names on them, 3 woman and 3 men. All of them had $100,000 in them. The envelopes had stamps on them too. Billy said, "We will have to see if we can locate these people, if they are alive, and forward this to them." He made another trip to the safe with the envelopes and now the box was empty. Billy and I went through 2 more boxes that day.

We didn't find anymore cash, but we did find love letters from a woman to Nick and they were not from Eddie. That sly devil. I looked at the name and said, "Billy, was one of the names on the envelope with the money in it addressed to Leslie Armstrong?" He looked up at me and said, "Yeah why?" I held up the love letter and he grabbed it. "Oh My God, he was cheating on Eddie." I pulled out more love letters from the other two ladies whose names were on the money envelopes. I handed them to Billy. He just shook his head and said, "This is just so wrong, Nick. What were you thinking?" I said, "Billy, do you still wanna look up those ladies and give them their money?" He said, "I will still try to find them, yes. Nick wanted us to go through all his stuff, so yes, I need to."

Billy did a lot of investigating and all the women had passed away. He asked a co-worker that worked with Wills and was told that since it was not listed in the Will, the money was ours to keep and do whatever we wished. We did not have to locate any of their survivors. Billy threw away the envelopes and added the money to our safe. He was still researching the mens names. We still had a ton of boxes to go through and figure stuff out before we did anything else.

We stopped to go get something to eat for dinner and came back and Billy brought in another box and it wasn't sealed. He opened it and said, "Aww. Look babe." I peeked over and looked in. They were wedding pictures of Nick and Edith Ford. Wow, they were really young. They looked like teenagers. We looked through the whole box and it was all photographs of him and Eddie and their vacations and their homes. It told their whole life in pictures and they were all in order until her death last year. Her death certificate was at the bottom. He put it there and never sealed the box. Billy added Nick's death certificate to the very bottom of the box. He said, "I am going to make a movie out of this. I don't know why, but I feel like I have to preserve his life for some reason." I smiled at him and said, "I love that idea." He marked the box "Pictures" and put it aside.

He pulled out the next one, which was sealed. It was full of newspaper articles and full copies of newspapers that were very, very old and yellowed and almost crumbly. He looked at the top of the paper to see a date. "1947" was the year and it was an obituary for 'Henry Ford'.

(1863-1947) We both looked at each other and Billy said, "WHAT THE FUCK? No, this can't be. This can't be right. Is he descendant of Henry Ford? Why would he have this?" He was very careful with that newspaper and he put it aside and kept looking. They were all newspaper articles relating to Henry Ford and all his relatives and his company and a bunch of obituaries from the Ford Family. "Holy Shit Em. This is where he got his money. His family was fucking rich. Somehow he is a relative. We just have to figure out how, if we can. So Nick was 75 and he was born in 1946, a year before Henry Ford died. I can't believe this. Do you really think this could be real?" I was still in shock and said, "I don't know babe. How did he get these newspaper articles? Were they given to him or did he order them and keep them all these years. We need to go through the box thoroughly and maybe we can tell how, if at all, he was related."

Billy was psyched now and wanted to keep going through boxes. He looked at me and said, "One more until tomorrow. I can't believe all this shit." I laughed at him and said, "You never know who your neighbors are." He scanned the boxes, trying to get the best one and pulled one out with no markings on it and said, "The last one I pulled out that wasn't marked, was awesome." He opened the box. It was full of baby pictures. A birth certificate at the top for a baby boy named James Nicholas Ford. He was born on May 22, 1970. Billy looked at me and I was looking at him. He said, "Nick said he didn't have any kids.

So this baby is 51 years old now. What the hell? Did Nick lie to us?" He stopped looking in the box and I think his feelings were hurt that Nick lied to him. I said, "Billy, you have to keep looking because you don't know the whole story. Let's keep looking. I don't think Nick lied to you." He was going really slow and he was bent over the box. I went in the kitchen and came out with a chair for him to sit on and went back for one myself. There were tons of baby pictures of Nick holding the baby and Eddie holding the baby and a couple of pictures of Eddie pregnant. Then, right after

James 4th birthday party, the pictures stopped and there were no pictures of any babies. Billy was digging through the box. "Billy, go in order and find out what the story is telling you." There was a letter to Nick from Eddie and it was in an envelope dated 1974, right after the 4th birthday party. It was mailed from Texas. The letter read:

Dear Nick:

I know you will never forgive me for what I've done, but I really do love you. I wanted a baby so bad that it drove me to this. I never loved James' father, I just wanted a baby. It was a one time thing, just one time, I swear to God. I want to come home, please, I beg you.

Love

Edith

Billy looked at me and said, "He didn't lie to me. It wasn't his kid. Oh my God." I said, "I told you I didn't think he lied. He was a good man Billy."

He went to the next letter that was from Nick
to Eddie.

Dear Eddie:

You may come home alone. I will not bring up
another man's child. I know that you want a
child and we will try, but I forbid that child in
my house because he is not mine. I know you
may think I am a mean man, but I am not. I do
love him, but he is not my flesh and blood. Let
me know what you decide.

Love,

Nick

Another letter after that from Eddie stated that
she would put the child up for adoption and
come home because she loved him. She said,
"I will never forgive myself for this because he
IS my flesh and blood."

The next paper was an adoption paper. James
was adopted by a man named Colt Warner
and his wife, from Michigan in 1975.

The next paper was heartbreaking and we both got tears in our eyes. It was a letter from James to Edith. He wanted to know why he was adopted and he told her that he remembered her and his birthday party. He told her he was happy with his adoptive parents, but would like to meet her and get some family history and that he would understand any story that she told him.

There as no letter from Eddie because she obviously wrote it back to him and then another letter from James thanking her for getting back to him. He told her he understood, but he wanted to get together at some point. That was the last letter from him and we don't know if she ever met with him.

Billy and I just sat there for a few moments, letting all this sink in and I was wondering if he was still alive and if he knew that she died. Billy said to leave it because it wasn't our business and he didn't want to stir up any trouble. I said to Billy, "That is why he cheated on her. I know 2 wrongs don't make a right, but he was probably hurt all his life about it and he took her back, but was probably unhappy."

The next few papers shocked the life out of us. Apparently, Nick did NOT cheat on his wife, even after all she did to him. The three women that were writing him love letters, was after her death. He met them at the casino (after her death). He started gambling when she died and met these three woman and he was just having fun with them. He wrote a letter to the box. (This box).

To whomever is reading this right now:

I never cheated on my wife. Never, Ever, Not even after her death. I never even kissed the women listed on those envelopes. I took them out on the town and bought them meals and gambled with them and bought them drinks and had fun and that is all. They knew I had money and that is all they were after. I think they were all sisters. When I came home from this vacation to Colorado, I received love letters, which I never responded to. These woman were much older than me and just

needed some company and fun and I gave
that to them and that is all. I was going to
send them some money, but they died. They
all died in the same car accident.

As far as James is concerned, I wasn't mad at
James, I was mad at Eddie for lying to me and
telling me that James was my son. We tried
for a child and it never happened and for that I
am sad. I was sad for Eddie and sad for
myself. I did contact James and apologized to
him and I spent some time with him and I did
give him money. It doesn't make up for what I
did, but I hoped that it helped him. I am not a
bad man, but I think I am being punished for
what I did, because now I have no one. Not
one person that will give me the time of day. I
have no family and all my friends are dead and
I live in a big house, all by myself. I wish I
could tell Eddie how sorry I am, but it's too late
for that. I made her give up something she
loved, her only child, and I am ashamed of
myself for it. I am done with this letter
because no matter what I write, it will not
make a difference.

Thank you to the person reading this and for listening to me. I am laughing now because no one will ever read this!

Billy and I were bawling by the end of this letter and Billy was having a hard time reading it out loud and had to stop a few times because he was sobbing for poor Nick.

I told Billy to keep going and do a few more letters so it would take his mind off Nick's sad letter for a while. I handed him a tissue and he agreed that we should keep going for a bit. I mean how much more shit could have happened? Ha-Ha.

Actually, there was one more letter under that one, in an envelope and it was a brand new one that was put there recently.

Dear Emily and Billy:

I am so grateful to have lived next door to you wonderful people. You made my last days very happy and you were both the very best friends that I could have asked for at this time in my life. I thank you for all the coffee dates with cake, the dinners and desserts, the breakfasts, our breakfast date at the diner and most of all your friendship and company. I envied the love between the both of you (It shows) and I hope you live happily ever after together. May God Bless you Both and stay healthy and happy. Forgive each other if needed and most of all, remember me always. It means a lot to me that you took me under your wings and treated me with respect and love.

Oh, I am not related to Henry Ford, just in case you read that box. I would like to think I was, but after a lot of research, I am just Nick Ford. I bet I had you going there for a minute. LOL.

Take care kiddos and enjoy your inheritance. You earned every cent.

Love you both,

Nick

XOXO

I still cried after reading this letter, but felt better than after the other one. Billy had a smile on his face and was happy.

We closed the box and went inside and brought the kitchen chairs back inside. Billy was quiet and started walking towards the shower. I came up behind him and pinched his butt and then rubbed his back. "We did a good thing Billy. A really good thing and I am proud and you should be too." He turned around and said, "I AM proud. I am. I just miss the old bugger. You don't think he ended his life do you? It's almost like he knew he was going to die." I shook my head and said, "I really don't know and I don't want to know."

21

BAD WEATHER AND MORE BOXES

We went in to take a shower and we had some really good sex in there. We headed for the bedroom and Billy turned on the TV and we watched the news to see what was going on. Nothing good and then we watched the weather. Looked like a bad rain storm coming. I drifted off to sleep.

The next morning, I woke up and Billy was gone. I smelled coffee and got up. I put my robe on and went down to the kitchen. Billy wasn't there, but he left a note. "Went to get some bagels and cream cheese. Be back in a few. I love you more than you know." I smiled at the note and put it near my heart. God how I loved this man.

I made myself a coffee and I heard his car drive in. He came in with the bagels and kissed me and dropped the bag on the counter. "Are you ready for another day of box hunting?" I said, "Yes, but let's bring the boxes in here, one at a time, so we are not breaking our backs. Mine is killing me today."

He said, "Oh, that's why mine hurts." He laughed and said, "We will look at them out in the patio if the rain holds off. That reminds me that I want to check the weather again because it said it was going to be a bad storm." He turned the TV on in the sitting room and I made some bagels and another coffee for Billy and brought it all in on a tray.

He smiled at me and said, "This is nice. Thanks." He leaned over and kissed me when I sat next to him. The weather was on and he said, "Uh oh, this bad rain storm is a hurricane. WTF? Can't they ever get anything right? We better go get a few cases of water and some rolls and cold cuts and some other things. Do you know what we need?" I told him we had 4 cases of water, cold cuts, rolls, bread and milk and plenty of produce and meat. "We don't have to go anywhere. We are all set and if you want anything extra, we can do an Instacart." He said, "Snacks, we need snacks." I laughed at him and told him we had a shit load of chips and ice cream and I could make some cupcakes or a cake or brownies if he wanted. He hugged me and said, "Have I told you lately how awesome you are?" I said, "No, you haven't actually. You can start anytime now." I was laughing. He said, "You are the best thing that has ever happened to me." He started fueling the fire and we got into it. Hot and heavy…

We stepped into the shower and got dressed in sweats and Billy went out into the garage and carried in 3 boxes. He said there were just a few left. He said, "I wonder what we will find today?"

He opened the first box and there was a receipt for a 1964 1/2 Ford Mustang. He bought it in 1964 and he paid $2,368.00. Wow. We will never see that again. There was a picture of it. It was a black Mustang and it had a hard-top. Attached to the receipt was an envelope with something in it. He opened the envelope and it was a key. Was this the key to the car? He examined it and it said Mustang on the key. Billy looked at me and said, "I am confused." The envelope underneath, said, "Raleigh Self Storage on McNeil Street". There was a key in the envelope. Billy said, "He has a storage unit and this is the key. I wonder what he has in there? We have to check this out right away because he isn't paying for it now." I looked at him and said, "Billy. I think it's his car. I really think he saved his car." His eyes lit up and he said, "You think so? Do you know what this means? Holy Shit Em." He took the envelope and the key we found attached to the picture of the car and said, "Let's go. I don't want to lose this if its his car." I got my purse and we went to the storage unit. We were met by a person that works there and they wanted to know why we were looking for Nick's unit. Billy told him that Nick had passed away and that we inherited everything. He introduced himself as Ned and told us that the unit was paid for until 2025 and took us to the unit. Billy was so nervous and his hand was shaking. Ned left us and I took the key from Billy and unlocked it. He lifted up the door and…Holy Shit…The car was in there and it was covered up. Billy pulled off the cover and it was like brand new. There wasn't a scratch on it, just some dust. Billy's eyes were bulging and he was emotional. "Oh My God." Was all he could say.

We both got in and sat in it for about 10 minutes. He put the key in the ignition and it started. Ned came by again and he told Billy that he was paid to come and start the car everyday and keep it in tip top shape. Billy just stared at him and said, "Really? He paid you to start it every day? Are you still being paid?" Ned told him that he received a lump sum of money to take care of the car until 2025 when the storage fees ended. Billy told him to keep up taking care of it until we decided what we were going to do with it.

Ned said, "You are one lucky couple to inherit all his stuff. He had a lot." Billy turned off the car and we all covered it up again. We locked up the storage shed and Billy put the keys on his keyring. He said, "And now we own an awesome Ford Mustang. Holy Shit."

We went home and continued looking through the box. He saw another piece of paper with a man's name on it. Matt Howard was the name. I looked at Billy and said, "That is one of the names on the envelope with the money in it." It was a receipt for a car that he purchased from Matt for $100,000. I said,

"That was the amount in the envelope. He never paid for the car." Billy was getting excited because attached to the receipt was a picture of the car he bought and an envelope with a key in it. The receipt was dated June 4, 1980. The car was a 1962, Jaguar E-Type. Then there was another Storage Unit with a key for the unit. Billy looked at me and said, "We now have a Jaguar and I am betting that those other 2 men on the envelopes with the money in them, are next. He bought cars from them all. But why didn't he give them the money for them? I am so confused." I was excited now and said, "Billy Keep going, keep going." He pulled out the next paper and it was a receipt dated June 4, 1980 for a 1985 Ferrari 288 GTO. I said, "Isn't that the same day he bought the Jaguar?" He looked and said, "Yeah. What the hell?" Then there was the picture of the red Ferrari and the key was attached and the storage unit with the key. The car was bought from Jerry Howard. I said, "Wait, Jerry Howard and Matt Howard? Oh My God, Keep going." The next one was… you guessed it, another receipt for the same day from Nathaniel Howard for $100,000. Those were the 3 men that were on the envelopes with the money in them. I wonder how we didn't notice they had the same last name? This car was a pale metallic green, 1976 Porche 930 Turbo and it was also in a storage unit and the key was there too. They were all in different storage units. They were all in Raleigh. That was the end of that box.

Billy closed the box and took all the keys, pictures and a copy of Nick's Will, so if he had to prove we inherited them, he could. We left for the first unit and same as with Ned, Nick had paid them to keep the car running and taken care of, until 2025.

All three cars were being taken care of by the owners of the storage units. We only had to show the Will to one place and they let us in. These storage units were all inside. You needed to get by the employee before entering to get to the unit. Billy told all of them to keep taking care of the cars until he decided what to do with them.

Since we only had a 2 car garage, we would need to either move to a larger house with lots of garages or rent garages to keep the cars in, or sell the cars. We had no idea what to do with any of this inheritance. I told Billy that our inheritance was a full time job and if we kept working, it would take us years to take care of everything. He agreed. We still had to figure out why these 3 men didn't get paid for their cars. Did they die? Were they brothers with the same last name?

We got home and I made 2 boxes of brownies and put it in a big pan. Billy loved his brownies and so did I.

The rain started and Billy went around closing everything down for the hurricane. We had hurricane shutters that were push button, so it was easy. He put new batteries in the flashlights and lanterns and fans and he brought some water in from the garage. He brought in a cooler and filled it with ice and started making ice. We should have done this earlier, but we still had some ice made in the garage freezer, so we were ok. Billy was so laid back when it came to this stuff and that made it comfortable for me. I have never been through a hurricane before and to be honest, I wasn't scared because of his demeanor.

I took the brownies out of the oven and let them cool before cutting them up. Billy came in and said, "I smell something good babe." He took a spoon out the drawer and dug in with the spoon. I told them they were hot, but that didn't matter to him. I laughed when he put it in his mouth and then danced around because they were hot. "Holy Shit that's hot." I just laughed at him and said, "You burned your mouth?" He spit it out in his hand and said, "YUP. Wow". He was blowing on it and then put it back in his mouth. He was a piece of work. Such a foodie.

The rain got bad and so did the wind, but Billy never even flinched to make me scared. I jumped when a branch flew off the tree in front and hit the shutter. We saw the dent from the inside. The wind was really scary and Billy looked at me and said, "You ok? Are you scared?" I told him I was a little scared and that I never went through a hurricane before. He grabbed me and brought me to the couch and held me tight and said, "Everything is fine, we are fine and you are fine. I won't ever let anything happen to you. I promise. We are totally safe. Don't be scared."

The storm went on through the night. We warmed up dinner in the microwave, that I had cooked the day before, which was chicken and rice casserole. We lost electricity after I heated up the last dish. Billy turned on the lanterns and put two on the dining room table.

He put one in the bathroom and one in the kitchen and then we each had one to carry around with us. We ate dinner and then just sat hugging each other on the couch and Billy had music playing from his phone. We went to bed and held each other for the remainder of the storm and we were fine. We woke up and still had no electricity when we got up. We had bagels and cream cheese and ice tea for breakfast. Better than nothing, I guess. I wanted coffee so bad and so did Billy.

We kept the freezers closed and hopefully we would get the electricity back before it defrosted. Billy put the milk, eggs and cold cuts in the cooler with the ice and a few other things that we didn't want to lose. He got more ice from the garage freezer and put it on top.

I told him that we should invest in a generator for the whole house and he laughed and said, "Yeah, I think we can afford it, but I wanted to talk to you about something today and get your feeling on it." I looked at him and said, "I think I know what your thinking". He said, "You do?" I said, "If I am right, you want to sell and buy bigger?" He looked shocked and said, "You really can read my mind." I said, "No, it just makes sense. We need room for the cars, if you want to keep them and although I love this house, we don't have that room." He smiled at me and said, "I love this house too and we don't have to sell it at all. We can just buy another one and one in Connecticut, thanks to Nick." He looked up and said, "Thanks Nick." He looked at me and said, "I want to keep the cars. I do. They were Nick's and I want them." I smiled and said, "And you shall keep them my love."

22

A NEW CHAPTER

He said, "I wanted to talk to you about something else and if you still say no, then no it is and I will never ask again." I knew what he was thinking and I don't know how, but I did. I said, "Ok, go ahead, I think I know, but go ahead." He looked shocked. He said, "You already know? Then what is your answer?" I said, "I have been thinking about it too and my answer is yes, I want to. I think I am ready for it." His whole face lit up and then he said, "Let's make sure we are on the same page here. You want to have a baby?" I laughed at him and said, "Yes, we are on the same page." He said, "I just hope it's not too late for us. What do you think?" I said, "Well, I am 26 and you are 30 and people have them later than that. I think we are ok. You have to have your vasectomy reversed or find out what you have to do. I think there is a way without having it reversed. I think it's called aspiration or something like that." He smiled and said, "You know who changed my mind?" I smiled and started to cry and said, "Yes, Nick did. He changed my mind too. I don't want to be alone with no one in my life, ever. He made me realize that, that can happen and I don't ever want to be that person."

We made it through the hurricane and we got our electricity back and we ate brownies until they were coming out of our ears. We did a lot of talking while we were sitting in the dark. We decided to keep this house because we loved it. We were looking for a house in Connecticut and Billy decided to do the reversal instead of the aspiration and his sperm count was going up and up. It takes a while and depends on how long ago you had the vasectomy. Of course, you only need one sperm. We were trying for our first baby. Yes, I said first baby. We decided to have two children, if it was in the cards for us. We didn't tell anyone what we were doing.

We both gave our notice at work and everyone was sad we were leaving. Billy promoted the top attorney to become partner and then Attorney Kaufman announced his retirement, so Billy had to promote two attorneys to take over the firm. I promoted Evelyn Lopez to become the Paralegal Manager because she was the best the office had and she was the best person for the job. I advertised for another paralegal for the office and I helped Evelyn interview. Once everything was in place, we both left. The office had a huge going away party for us and they were sad to see us go.

We were starting another chapter in our lives and I was so excited. We were looking for another house in North Carolina. It had to be big enough (bedroom wise) and had to have enough garage space for at least 6 cars. Those cars meant a lot to Billy and I wasn't going to stand in his way.

Now that we left our jobs, Billy started looking up the Howards to see if they were brothers or cousins or what. We needed to know if we had to send the money to them for the cars or what. But we also had to go through the rest of the boxes to see if there was anymore information on the Howards before we gave them anything. It's a good thing we went through the boxes first, because we found out that they were gamblers. Nick wanted to buy their cars and he put the money up front for them at the poker table in the envelopes with their names on them. It turns out that they gambled their cars away, so Nick got them fair and square and didn't owe them anything.

Billy took the money out of the envelopes and put it in the safe and threw away the envelopes. One more thing out of the way and we didn't need to find out if they were brothers or cousins. It didn't matter to us, who they were.

We found a beautiful house in Connecticut, right near the beach. If we were right on the beach, we would have to have a cottage, so we opted for the house and it was close enough to walk to the beach. It was huge and looked like a mansion, but it wasn't. It was gorgeous inside and had everything we needed, plus guest rooms, so my family, or Billy's family could stay with us if they wanted to. My family was 40 minutes inland, which isn't bad. We paid cash for the house, which made the closing easy. We visited with my parents and catered a dinner while we were there and had my brothers and families over too. We got to see the new kitties and they were adorable.

Billy and I gave my parents $100,000 and my mom almost had a heart attack. We gave Jesse and Jack each $100,000 and Jesse collapsed on the floor from shock. He didn't pass out, but he was in shock.

We told everyone that we just bought a house on the beach and Nick left us tons of money and cars and other things. We told them that we still had boxes to go through, so there was still stuff that we didn't know about. It has been almost a year that he passed away and it has taken us this long to get where we are. We told them that we quit our jobs, but we never told them that we were trying for a baby. That would be another visit.

Billy picked up Haley and was cuddling with her and talking to her. "Boy You are getting big. You are such a big girl now." He was kissing her and hugging her. He was totally different towards her now and I could see that he was ready.

Jesse and Maria announced that they were pregnant that day and we were all excited to hear the news. She was three months along, but you couldn't see a bump yet. I asked Jack if he was going to have another and he told us they were trying.

Our family was growing and I was hoping I could add to that news soon. We had a nice weekend with everyone and then flew back home.

We had a catered dinner at our house for Billy's family and did the same thing. We gave his parents $100,000 and each of his sisters $100,000. Everyone was in shock as usual. We told them that we bought a house in Connecticut and that we quit our jobs, to which his mom screamed, "YOU WHAT?" His father put his hand on her leg and said, "Shut it". Billy said, "Mom, calm down. You have no idea how much Nick left us and we still have more stuff to go through. We have his original 1964 Ford Mustang, along with 3 other cars that he won in a poker game. At the time that he won them, they were worth $100,000 and god knows what they are worth now. We sold his house, we have collectors items from his wife, we have bank accounts, CD's, Money market accounts, retirement accounts and savings accounts, not to mention envelopes full of money in boxes. You have no fucking idea. So yes, we quit our jobs and we gave you money and Em's parents and brother's money and we bought a house near the beach in Connecticut. We are going to buy a bigger house here too, so I can house the cars." His dad said, "So you are keeping the cars?" Billy said, "Dad, I can't wait to show you these cars. Your eyes will pop out of your head. They are awesome and yes, I am keeping them." His dad shook his head and he had a smile on his face and said, "I can't wait to see them." He smiled at his dad and said, "Can you believe that Nick bought the Mustang for $2,368.00?" His father was in shock and said, "Holy Crap really?" Billy shook his head yes and said he had the receipt for it. His father laughed and said, "The receipt alone is probably worth money." The both of them were talking up a storm and my brother-in-laws were listening in and his Dad was really interested in cars, so he was listening intently.

I was telling his mom and sisters about Eddie's collections of ancient china and her coin collections. "We haven't had a chance to even check on those things yet. It has taken us this long to figure out all this so far, but now that we aren't working, it should start to go faster.

It took us 6 months to get his house cleaned out, because he had so much stuff and there were safe's in floor boards. You have no idea. Even when we thought we went through the whole house, we kept thinking we missed something." I laughed and then said, "I bet we forgot something or left something important." Anna wanted to know what we were doing with this house and we told her we were keeping it because we both loved it. She said, "That doesn't make sense. You should just sell it." Dan put his hand on her leg again and said, "Shut it". I saw Billy smirk and turn his head away and then he turned towards her and said, "Mom, Em and I love this house and we are keeping it. It is our first house and we can afford to keep it, so we are." She smiled at him and said, "Ok, I get it."

His sister Sarah announced that she was pregnant with a little boy and was 4 months and that they didn't have a name yet. Anna went ballistic because this would be her first grandchild. We all congratulated her.

I felt sorry for Liz, but she seemed fine. I gave her a little tug and hugged her. She whispered to me, "*I am fine, don't worry about me. We are actually in the adoption process.*" I hugged her and whispered back "*I am so happy for you.*" We all cleaned up and I sent everyone home with food.

23

IS THIS A JOKE?

Billy and I continued to try for a baby and the doctor said, "It will take time because your sperm count has to grow." That was 4 months ago. I was praying it would happen soon because the longer it took, the older we were getting.

I woke up to the smell of coffee and got up. I put on my robe and went down to the kitchen. Billy was feeding the cats and they were making a racket because they were hungry. They were so friggin cute and they were

rubbing on his legs as he was adding the wet food to their dishes. Billy pointed to the counter. "I made you coffee babe." I used my nose and followed the smell. LOL. "Oh thanks babe." I sat at the counter and he came over with his coffee. "I found a house" He was fiddling with his phone trying to bring up the picture. He showed me and I about fell off my stool. "Oh MY. Billy that is exquisite.

How many cars does that garage fit? It looks like a house." He laughed and said, "It is an 8 car garage. It has a storage house on the property for lawnmowers and stuff. It has 6 bedrooms, 2 offices, 4 baths, a pool, a hot tub, a screened patio, a laundry room, a sitting room, a living room, a huge kitchen, a kitchen on the lanai, 3 acres of land, a flower garden, a picnic area with a table and a lot of other stuff. Here look at all the pictures. It's 800,000."

I looked at all the pictures and said, "Let's go look at it." I sipped my coffee and all of a sudden, I felt sick to my stomach. I ran for the bathroom and threw up the coffee. I cleaned up and brushed my teeth and smiled in the mirror. I think I am pregnant because this has never happened to me before.

I took a test out of the drawer and took it. Billy knocked at the door. "Are you ok Em?" I said, "Come in." I wiped off the stick and put it on the counter. He looked at me and said, "Did you get sick?" I smiled and said, "Yes, I did." We both stared at the stick and stared at the stick and then…it said positive. Billy looked at me and said, "Oh My God. This is really it. We did it. There is no turning back now." He hugged me and said, "Oh EM, I am so friggin happy. You have no idea." I looked at him and said, "No turning back now? Did you change your mind." He took me by the shoulders and said, "It's a figure of speech hon. I couldn't be happier than I am right now. You have made me a happy man." We hugged. He said, "Do you still wanna go see the house today?" I shook my head yes and said, "Let's go." He said, "We will stop somewhere for breakfast. Take a plastic bag in case you get sick and no more caffeinated coffee for you."

He took me out for breakfast and I ordered a decaf coffee and had scrambled eggs and toast and I was fine. My new item to carry around was a plastic bag in case I got sick. Billy had one in his pocket at all times too.

We made an appointment to see the house and it was for 2:00 p.m. We drove around the neighborhood to see what it was like and it was beautiful. It was in Durham, North Carolina and that is only 26 miles from Raleigh. We saw the house and it was absolutely gorgeous and we put in an offer for $750,000.

They snapped at it and I guess it was the very first offer they had. Holy Shit. We just bought another house. This was a great deal for what we got, because we looked around and the same house with the land, was going for over a million dollars. We made out really good.

We shopped for furniture for days and days and had it delivered. Billy arranged for the transport of all 4 cars to our garage. We got one a day for 4 days. It just happened that way. We spent most of our time at the new house because we had a lot of deliveries happening and we took our kitties with us. We got our bed, living room and shower stuff first so we would be all set. The cats did a lot of scouting around. There was nothing they could get into so they were safe. We ordered all the beds for the other bedrooms and desks and shelving for the offices. We ordered TV's, coffee tables, a dining room set, washer and dryer, a freezer for out in the garage, a generator for the whole house, patio furniture and pool furniture.

We set the whole place up and all the cars were delivered and in their own bays. We bought a safe and had it installed and put all the paperwork in it for the cars and receipts for everything we bought and for the sale of the house. I bought area rugs, foot rugs, welcome rugs, new hand towels, washcloths, sheets, bath towels and everything else we needed. I bought dishes, silverware, pots and pans and all the kitchen stuff needed. I was going to have to do this again for the Connecticut house. We finally finished with our new house and everything was in place. I did a huge Instacart and got food for the house to the tune of $500.00, which really wasn't bad considering there was nothing in the house.

I was still getting sick, first thing in the morning with the first sip of coffee, but after that, I was fine. I made an appointment with my gynecologist and he confirmed my pregnancy and gave us a due date of September 29th. The ultrasound was scheduled for April 19th. Billy was getting so excited and he wouldn't let me lift anything heavier than 5 lbs. He kept asking me "Are you ok Em?" He did most of the cooking these days because he didn't want me to stand too long. I told him that I can still do it, but near the end is the important part when I wouldn't be able to stand too long. He also took me out to eat a lot too. We went to our favorite restaurants in Chapel Hill and we checked on our other house daily.

He hired a housekeeper for our new house and he had a landscaper and a pool guy. He started all of his cars every day. He told me he was going to have the Mustang looked at and have all the hoses and everything replaced. He wanted to take it for a ride.

He had a car guy come out and look at it and he told him that it looked like everything was new in it. "They must have replaced everything already. It's in tip top shape Dude." Billy tried to pay the guy, but the guy told him that just seeing the car was payment enough and he wouldn't take a dime. He also looked at the other cars while he was there and he said they were awesome and didn't need anything and he offered to come and take care of them anytime he needed something. He said, "These cars are the bomb Dude. Anything you need and I will be here." Billy thanked him.

We had one more month before we could tell anyone, but Billy wanted to wait until we found out the sex and then tell everyone. The morning sickness was subsiding. It only happened a couple times a week now and I couldn't wait till it stopped. The doctor said it should stop by the end of the first trimester and it did. Thank God. I had a small belly and not really noticeable. It was only noticeable to me because my pants were tight. I only gained 5 lbs so far.

Our ultrasound date was here. We were both so excited to find out the sex of the baby. We were in the room and the sonographer came in and she was all smiles and so cheerful. She did her testing and then looked up and said, "Do you want to know the sex of the baby?" Billy said, "Yes, yes we do." I shook my head yes. She pointed to a place on the screen and said, "There it is, the little mushroom, as I call it." She started laughing. "You are having a little boy. Congratulations." Billy looked at her and said, "Really? We are having a boy?" She assured him we were having a boy. He looked at me and said, "OH EM, we are having a baby boy. OH Em." He couldn't believe it. She told us that the baby looked healthy and was growing perfectly.

We drove home and Billy kept looking at me and said, "Oh EM. I am so proud." When we got home he took the pictures that we got and took a picture of one of them and sent it to everyone in the family. "Please welcome our new male addition, coming your way around September 29th." Our phones were silent for more than 30 minutes. No one answered us at all, not even my mom. Finally, Jack texted back and said, "Is this a joke?" Billy said, "No joke. We are pregnant with a little boy and Em is due September 29th." No response. He must have fallen off his chair. LOL. Then my mom texted Billy. "Are you playing a joke on us, because this is not funny. Where did you get that picture?" Billy started cracking up and he couldn't even text back. "Everyone thinks it's a joke Em, and they think I am playing around, so you better send it. I attached the picture and said the following: "ATTENTION EVERYONE... THIS IS NOT A JOKE...I am pregnant with a little boy and I am due on September 29th." Billy had his vasectomy reversed and we are planning on 2 children."

My phone went Berserk. Then Billy's phone went Berserk. Everyone was so excited and apologized for not responding but they all thought it was a joke. My mom could not believe it. She called me, "Honey, oh honey, I am so happy. I can't believe this. You didn't say anything to me about it." I told her that we didn't say anything to anyone about it because we weren't sure if it was going to work. I explained that even though it was reversed, didn't mean it would work, so we didn't want to get our hopes up or anyone else's.

We invited Billy's parents and sisters and family to see the house and have dinner with us the following Sunday. Everyone loved the house and Billy, his dad and his brother-in-laws all disappeared into the garage for over an hour. I went out to announce that the food had arrived and they all came in. Dan couldn't stop talking about the cars and said they were all stunning, but his favorite was the Mustang. It was Billy's favorite too.

We all had a nice dinner and everyone was talking about how nice the house was and how nice we decorated it. Everyone congratulated us on the baby and Sarah was doing well with her pregnancy. She had 2 months to go and they had no name yet or they weren't telling anyone. We picked a name and Billy wanted to tell everyone because he was so proud of it. He hit his fork on his glass and said, "A HEM. We picked a name for the baby and we want to announce it." He chuckled a little and his dad said, "Ok go ahead. You have our attention." Billy said, "His name is going to be Nicholas William Emerson. What do you think?" His Dad said, "That is a mighty fine fitting name for him and I love it." His mom said, "Don't you think…". All I heard was "SHUT IT". Everyone giggled and she said, "Sorry, there I go again. I love it too." Everyone said their goodbyes and left.

24

SECRET COMPARTMENTS

We were planning on staying the whole weekend at our old house so we could go through another couple boxes and be done with them. We packed up the cats and took some of the produce and a few things to make dinner with so it wouldn't go bad and we left. It only took us 15 minutes. We weren't far at all.

We opened a few windows to air the place out and then closed them up and got the cats situated and gave them food and water. Billy got a box and brought it in. We sat in the sitting room and he opened it.

The first envelope had a piece of paper that looked like plans to his house and showed his front door with 6 panels. Billy looked at me and said, "Holy Moly, we missed something at the house." I said, "What did we miss?" He said, "According to these plans, there as a secret sliding door in the panel of his front door. I mean, I don't know if there is anything in there, but why would he have it, if he didn't plan on putting something in there?" He kept looking and the back door had one too. He said, "What do we do? I mean, we can't just go next door to the new neighbor and say, "We forgot something in a secret compartment. Maybe we can wait and see if they remodel or something and then just take the doors." I said, "I wonder what he put in there? This guy had so much going on, so it could be anything." Billy said, the safe under the floor board was in the plans but we already knew about that one.

There was a brown envelope underneath the plans for the first floor. It was plans for the second floor. There were secret compartments in the walls behind the built-in dressers in all three bedrooms.

The last envelope contained the plans for the basement. There were two secret compartments down there too. Billy said, "Why didn't he let us know all this before we sold the house?" I looked at Billy and said, "You know what Billy? Whatever it was, is still there and we can't be greedy. Look what he gave us in return for one month of friendship

and company." He smiled at me and said,
"You are right Em. Look what we have
already."

He brought in the last two boxes and said,
"This is it. I want to be done with boxes."
Neither one of the boxes were marked and
they were sealed. He pulled it open and there
were 2 old tin boxes that looked like old
lunchboxes that a child would take his lunch to
school in, but slightly bigger. He opened the
first one and there was a ton of money just
stacked in there. $100's, $50's, $10's and $5's
and we were counting it and it totaled $50,000.
Billy sat there and didn't move for a minute. I
looked at him and said, "You ok?" He said,
"Yeah, but look at this box and look at that
one" and he pointed to one of Nick's boxes
that he had put up on a shelf with his wedding
photos in it. I don't think these were Nick's
boxes. These boxes are really old. They don't
look like Nick's boxes. The bills are old. Look
at the dates on them. He took out the other
lunchbox and that was loaded with $1,000's
and there was $75,000 in that box and the bills

were really old and it looked like some of them were worth some money. Billy said, "Where did you get these boxes from?" I explained that they were in the basement under a sliding door and told him where. Billy said, "I bet Nick didn't even know this was there. They weren't Nick's." He showed me the plans for the basement and said, "Show me whereabouts you found them." I looked at the plans and said, "Right here" and I pointed. I told him the door was open a little at the bottom and I slid it up and found the two boxes. Billy shook his head and said, "Yeah, these boxes were there before Nick bought the house. That sliding door is not even in the plans he had. This is so crazy."

He pulled the last box towards him and it had 4 more lunchbox type tin boxes in it and they were full of old money too. He put all the money in shoe boxes that I had in the closet and put it in the safe. He saved the lunchboxes and pulled the cardboard box apart to search it, but didn't find anything and he threw it in the trash. "We are done with boxes. This was an adventure and a half." I looked at him and said, "You can say that again." And so he did and laughed at me.

He looked up at the box that was on the shelf with Nick's wedding pictures in it and said, "I still want to make a movie with those pictures so it will preserve them. If I leave them in that box, they will wither away." I smiled at him and said, "Do it Billy. Do it." He took the box down and the baby pictures box and brought them inside. He started Googling for someone to do the job. He found a couple of companies and then saw a guy that does it on the side and contacted him. The guy came out to the house the next day and Billy showed him the box full of stuff, plus the box of baby pictures. He asked who it was and Billy said, "He was my adopted Grandpa." The guy said he would do it for us and said he would put some nice music to it for $300.00. Billy told him to please take care of the box and not to let anything happen to the photographs or the box they were in. The guy was licensed and insured and gave Billy his card. His name was Carmen Loister and he told us that he would have it done by next weekend. Billy looked at him and said, "Please, please don't let anything happen to this." Carmen promised.

Carmen called Billy during the week and asked if he wanted the letters in the movie about the baby and the adoption and all of it and Billy told him that he wanted everything in it.

As promised, Carmen came back with the boxes full of photos and a CD of the movie. We put it in the CD player and watched the whole thing and it was so awesome. Carmen said, "Are you happy with it?" Billy said, "I am and thank you for doing this so fast." He gave him $400.00 cash and then asked him if there was a way to preserve the stuff in the box. Carmen gave him the name of a special paper to buy, but he offered to do it for Billy and Billy told him to do it and he would pay him for it. Carmen told him the paper was a little bit expensive but Billy told him to go ahead and we would pay him for it and to save his receipts. Carmen took the boxes back and came back with them the following weekend and Billy looked inside and couldn't believe what a nice job he did. All the photos were enclosed in some kind of case with paper around them. Carmen told him that the photos would last forever. He gave Billy the receipts and charged him $400.00 so Billy gave him $300.00 for the cases and paper and $500.00 for the job. Carmen handed him another business card and told him he would be happy to do any other work that Billy had. We both thanked him and he left.

We got a call the next day that Sarah was in labor and it wouldn't be long. Billy looked at me and said, "Wanna go to the hospital with me?" I said, "Yes, of course I do. Let's go." He had the biggest smile on his face and on the way to the hospital, he looked at me and said, "I am gonna be an Uncle again. I am so excited." I smiled at him and I was thinking that in a couple months, he was gonna be a Daddy and I was gonna be a Mommy. Holy Shit. Am I really ready for this? I hope I will be a good mother because I never had any experience at all on how to take care of a baby. I never even changed a diaper. I was getting a little anxiety and my hands started shaking. They say that motherhood comes naturally and you automatically know what to do. I will just go with that and pray that it happens to me.

We got to the hospital and we met the whole family in the waiting room. Anna came up to me and hugged me and then kissed my belly. "I am so excited for all my grandchildren." Billy had his arm around me. He treated me like a queen. I mean, he always did anyway, but now, he was attentive 24 hours a day to my every need and he checked on me all the time. He found two chairs next to each other and he made me sit and he sat next to me. He found a chair with arms for me so I could get up easier and he sat on the inside chair. He held my hand the whole time we waited for news on Sarah.

Sarah's husband, Mike, came through the door like a whirlwind and announced the birth of his son, Michael James Hewitt, Jr. He was 7lbs 8oz and 22 inches long and no hair. Mike had very light brown, almost blonde hair and Sarah had dark brown. Mike said, "Grandparents first please." Anna and Dan smiled at all of us and hurried in to see Sarah and their first grandchild and Mike's parents were there as well and they headed in. Billy was bouncing his leg, going a mile a minute, with nerves. I put my hand on his leg and said, "You ok?" He smiled at me and said, "Yeah, I can't wait."

Anna and Dan came out smiling as did Mike's parents. We were next with Liz and her husband, Joe. Billy grabbed the baby as soon as he got in the room and Sarah and Mike were all smiles. He hugged the baby and said, "Oh My God, I love him so much. Congrats you guys. I am so happy for both of you." I smiled at Billy. He was so ready to be a dad. Billy handed the baby to me and I sat in the chair first because I was nervous. Billy knew it and he said, "You will be fine. Just relax." He smelled so good. He smelled like a baby. I hugged him and I felt some motherly instincts kicking in. It's true, it's really true. It comes naturally. I am gonna be fine. "He is beautiful, just beautiful." I called Liz, "Your turn hon. Oh My God, he is gorgeous." She took him like a pro and Joe was looking on and then he took him and held him. We didn't stay long because Sarah needed to rest. Liz told me on the way out that the adoption would be final in a couple of months and that her and Joe were very excited. I hugged her and told her I was excited for her. She asked how I was feeling and I told her I was fine and doing good. I had 2 months to go and I felt fine, so far.

We had given Sarah a baby shower a couple of months ago and Billy told Mike that he and Joe would go put the crib together for him and do anything else he needed. Mike was thankful for that and thanked both of them. Sarah was coming home tomorrow, so we ordered food to be delivered. That way Mike wouldn't have to worry about serving anything. We had it all set up and Joe and Liz helped us. We put some blue balloons on their mailbox and had some inside too. We set up a folding table and put a blue table cloth on it and we decorated everything in blue. We set up the food on that table, along with soda, cups and ice. The kitchen had an ice bucket, whiskey, Tequila, Amaretto, (Sarahs favorite), sour mix, Vodka, lemons and limes, etc. Me and Billy ordered a cake and we ordered a jug of coffee from Dunkin and Joe went to pick it up. Billy and Joe put the crib together and Liz and I put a sheet on the mattress and put the comforter and blanket and bumpers in there with his new

Teddy Bear and put the mobile up. We set up his bassinet with sheets and a blanket. Everything was all set for Sarah and Mike.

The look on their faces when they came through the door with the baby, was priceless and Sarah started crying. "Thank you so much guys. This means the world to me." Mike guided her to a recliner and put the baby in the bassinet and tucked him in. We had a nice afternoon. Everyone ate and drank and Sarah even took a nap in the recliner. They had a lot of visitors during the day. Aunts and uncles from both sides of the family, the grandparents, cousins and immediate family. We cleaned everything up and left them to rest.

Billy and I drove home and he started fueling the fire in the car and continued fueling the fire when we got home, until the fire was roaring. We showered and got into bed. "How are you feeling Em? You never complain about anything. Are you ok?" I smiled at him and said, "I feel fine. I am just nervous about being a good mom and worried that I won't know what to do when the baby gets here. Like really nervous about that." He smiled at me and said, "It will all fall into place and you will know what to do instinctively and I will be here not knowing what to do either, right by your side." He started laughing. I laughed with him and said, "I hope between the two of us, we can figure it out."

I looked at him and remembered back when I met him at The Fresh Market and we lost our cars in the parking lot and we were both embarrassed, but we figured it out and got help. I said, "Remember when we both lost our cars in the parking lot? Remember when we went to Dunkin and you bought me coffee and breakfast? Remember the Chinese Lantern Festival and State Market?" He hugged me and said, "I will never forget that, ever. How can I forget that? You fueled my fire when I looked at you on the sidewalk and it's been going strong since then." I said, "Really? You never told me that." He looked surprised and said, "Are you sure I never told you? Well, maybe I never told you that exact scenario, but I have showed you many, many times. You fuel my fire every time I look at you. You are the love of my life."

The next day, we went back to our old house to check on things and saw a "For Sale" sign on Nick's old house. We looked at each other and right away Billy said, "The secret compartments!" I laughed at him. "I wonder why they are selling so soon?" He said, "Let's take a walk over and say 'hi'. We walked over and a lady answered the door. "Hi, can I help you? Oh, you are the people that sold us the house? You live next door?" Billy said, "We own the house next door, but we actually bought another house about 20 miles from here and we come to check on this house all the time. Is everything ok? We saw that you put it up for sale. I am not being nosey, just concerned," She put her hand out to shake hands with us and said, "I'm Madge, Come in". We walked in and it looked exactly as we sold it. They did nothing to the place. We introduced ourselves again and she took us to the kitchen where we all took a seat. She said, "My husband died a month ago and I don't want to live in this big house alone, so my son asked me to live with him and we put the house up for sale." Billy and I looked at each other and Billy said, "Oh, I am so sorry for your loss. I feel so bad." She smiled at Billy and said, "I am fine, really. My son will take care of me. He doesn't want me to live alone." Billy said, "If there is anything we can do for you, please don't hesitate to ask us." She thanked us and then she looked at me and said, "Congratulations. I see you have a baby on the way. It's so wonderful. What are you having or do you not know?" I told her we were having a little boy.

We had a nice visit with Madge and Billy asked if he could look around. He told her we might buy it back, but we weren't sure. (It was just an excuse) She looked surprised and said, "We never had a chance to do anything because my husband got sick, but feel free to look around." We went down to the basement and Billy checked the secret compartments and there was nothing there. We came right back up and we went upstairs to check behind the built-in dressers and there was nothing there so we just walked around. Billy said, "Yeah, it looks exactly as we left it." He was eyeing the front door and he winked at me. I think that

was my cue to take her back into the kitchen.
I walked into the kitchen and said, "Do you
mind if I just sit down for a second?"

She followed me into the kitchen and said, "Oh
of course not. It's hard to carry around
another human being." I sat in the chair and a
minute later, I saw Billy in the doorway. "We
have taken enough of your time Madge and
thank you for letting us look around. I
appreciate it. Let us know if you need
anything" He handed her a piece of paper with
his cell number on it. "You ready babe?" I got
up and we thanked Madge again and we left.
We walked next door and as we were walking
he said, "Nothing in either door. Either they
found whatever it was, or there was nothing."
I looked at him and said, "I don't think there
was anything and if there was, Nick probably
moved it to a box. We are done Billy. There
are no more secrets, no more boxes to go
through, no more secret compartments and
nothing more to do. It's time to move on to the
next Chapter in our life." He tugged at me and
hugged me and said, "I am ready for our next
Chapter."

Billy and I decided to wait, before going up to the Connecticut house, until after the baby came. I was too far along to be doing anything. We had to buy tons of furniture and all the necessities. Billy gave the keys to Jesse and Jack and asked them to take turns checking on the house for us. He told them if they wanted to stay there, they could, but there was no furniture yet. They agreed to check on it for us.

25

WELCOME TO THE WORLD

I had one month left to go and I was still feeling ok, but I was getting Braxton Hicks and it was scaring Billy. We had the baby's room all set. We had the bassinet in our room and Billy set up the diapers, wipes, onesies, sheets, blankets and the dressing table in our bedroom for now, so it would be more convenient for the both of us.

My mom and dad were on call and they would hop a plane as soon as Billy told them I was ready. They were going to stay and help. Phew…Thank God… Someone who knew how to take care of a baby. I felt so much better now that I knew my mom was going to be here. Billy leaned over me and said, "You ok? I see steam rising. I know you are worried, but everything is going to be ok and your mom will be here to help and so will my mom. You will have a lot of help. Mr. Nick is almost here." I smiled up at him and said, "I feel better that my mom is coming. I am still getting these Braxton Hicks and they are really strong." He said, "Are you timing those?" I shook my head no and said, "I still have 3 weeks babe." He laughed and said, "Well, Nick has other plans. I am calling your parents just in case and then the doctor." He called the doctor first and the doctor told him to bring me in just to be safe. Then he called my parents and my mom got so excited. "OHHHH. OK, we will be right there." I think she forgot she was in Connecticut. Billy was laughing at her. They drove to the airport and got tickets and they were on their way. Billy grabbed our packed bags, fed the cats, and took me to the hospital. The doctor checked me out and they were in fact, Braxton Hicks and I was not dilated, so they sent me home. False Alarm. I told him to leave the packed bags in the car. Billy laughed and looked up and said, "Stop playing tricks on me Nick."

My parents came that afternoon and settled into their bedroom upstairs and my mom was all bouncy and excited. She made dinner for everyone. I told her about my anxiety and how worried I was and I started to cry. She hugged me and said, "Wait until he arrives. You will know exactly what to do and you will be an excellent mother. Trust me. I had the same anxiety and everything just came naturally. I don't think I did a bad job, Do you?" I hugged her so tight and said, "I love you mom. You did an awesome job. I am so happy you are here for me." She said, "You are my blessing baby and you always will be."   I told her that Billy was making a joke about being right here by my side and not knowing what to do either and she laughed. She said, "Your father was the same way. Do you think you guys are the only ones that are scared about having a baby? Everyone goes through this."

As usual, my mom made me feel 100% better and my Braxton Hicks actually stopped. I think I was getting them because I was nervous. Billy made brownies while my mom was cooking and I watched a game on TV with my Dad and I snuggled up to him and put my head on his shoulder. This is something I haven't done in a long time and he loved it. I fell asleep on him and Billy took a picture on his phone. My mom took care of everything while I was sleeping. She set the table, cooked and directed Billy to get certain things for her, because she didn't know where things were.

Anna and Dan came to visit that night to see how things were going and I think Anna got a little jealous that my mom and dad were there. My mom was so sweet to her and always treated her with respect and she knew all the problems we had with her in the beginning. I mean, she didn't kiss her ass or anything, but she also didn't want any trouble with her and wanted to get along with her because we were all family now.

She served brownies and coffee and told Anna that they were staying to help out and to visit. Anna was fine and didn't start anything and Dan kept her in line these days. He would look at her and say Shut IT and she stopped whatever she was doing or saying. She did not want to lose her son again. Billy catered to me and kept asking about the contractions and seeing if I was ok.

He told his mother that I never complained, not once, about anything. She smiled at me and said, "How are you feeling hon?" I told her I was fine and just wanted it to be over. She said, "I hear ya. The end is so uncomfortable. But look at you, you didn't gain much weight did you?" I told her I gained 25 pounds and for me, that was a lot. She told me that 25 is normal, even for me. My mom was right by my side and she was rubbing my back. She and Billy were so attentive.

I hung around for one more week and it was 2 weeks before my due date. My water broke in the bathroom and I called Billy. He came flying in and took care of me and he called the doctor and told him we were on our way. The contractions started on the way to the hospital. We were 20 minutes away and I had 2 contractions. I never timed them, but I figured about 10 minutes. Then when we pulled into the emergency room, I got another one. Everything happened so fast. Before I knew it, I was in a hospital bed with a gown on and the contractions were close and strong, to the point of sickness. Billy was holding my hand and feeding me ice chips and kissing my face. He was talking to me in a calm soft voice and he was telling me how good I was doing. They gave me an epidural and then the sickness stopped and the pain was not as bad.

Two hours later, I gave birth to Nicholas William Emerson.   He was 8 lbs 3 oz and 21 inches long. He had a little bit of brown hair. Billy cut the cord and he was holding his son and he had tears in his eyes. "I have a son, a son named Nick and he is beautiful. Look at him Em. Look at him." He brought the baby to me and laid him on my chest. I felt it, I felt the motherhood kicking in. It does come natural. I held him and kissed him and I was instantly in love. The nurses took him away to clean him up and do their thing. Billy kissed me all over my face and said, "You make beautiful babies Em." I kissed him and said, "WE make beautiful babies Billy." He said, "You feel ok? Do you hurt? Can I do something for you?" The doctor stitched me up and they cleaned me up and they gave me something for pain. I fell asleep and when I woke up, Billy was sitting in the chair with his son. He smiled up at me and said, "Thank you Em. Thank you." He brought me the baby and we took a selfie of all 3 of us. I held the baby while he sent the picture and announcement to everyone in the family. "ATTENTION EVERYONE: THIS IS NOT A JOKE…. Our son, Nicholas William Emerson has arrived. He weighs 8 lbs 3 oz and is 21 inches long. He was born on September 15th at 3:10 p.m. I repeat. THIS IS NOT A JOKE." He was laughing and then showed me what he wrote. I started laughing and said, "Oh my God Billy. You are too much. I love you so much." He said, "Well, I didn't want them to ignore me." His phone blew up and everyone was congratulating us and telling us how beautiful he was. The next day, my room was filled with flowers galore. Billy went out to get food for us a couple times and he went home to shower, but came right back. My mom and dad came, his mom and dad came and everyone else met us at home the next day.

My brothers came down with their families and we had room for everyone. My mom got everyone settled into their rooms, she ordered food and cake and balloons and they had a little baby shower for us. I shouldn't say little because we go so much stuff. Nick got a lot of clothes, diapers, bibs, socks, onesies and undershirts and sneakers, Blankets, a monitor and numerous other gifts. I was so sore with the stitches, but I didn't have to do anything, except sit. Billy bought me a rocking chair that was upholstered and it was the most comfortable chair ever. He put a bow on it and put it in the living room. That is where I sat most of the day.

Nick was a good baby. He didn't cry much, except when he was hungry or had gas. I think I turned out to be a good mom and Billy was a good dad.

My mom was right, as usual. It comes to you naturally when you give birth. I knew how to change a diaper and burp and dress and rock. I did it all and I didn't need any instructions and neither did Billy.

When Nick was 7 months old, we took a trip to Connecticut and we started buying furniture for the house. We stayed with my parents while we were getting the house ready and waiting for furniture deliveries, including another crib and all the trimmings. We fixed a few things, like the garage door, some stone that was coming loose on the sidewalks, and we painted, actually touched up some areas that needed it. We stayed with my parents for 3 weeks and finally we were ready to move in. We stayed for 2 months during the summer months so we could enjoy the beach and then we left to go home to Raleigh.

Even though we loved our first house, we decided that it was best to sell it, because it was too much to handle and we were hardly ever there. We packed everything up and had it moved to our new home and we had plenty of room for everything. How do you fall in love with a house? Well, we did, but it was not serving a purpose anymore and we were doing the right thing. I cried the day we closed on it. Billy kept asking me if I was sure and I kept saying yes, because I knew we had to, but I didn't want to. It was our first house together and we met Nick there. But now we were in a new chapter of our life and we had to let it go.

That fall, I got pregnant again (on purpose). We had a little girl and we named her Elise Elizabeth Emerson. YUP EEE. We called her Lise for short. Two months after she was born, Billy went back and had his vasectomy again. Two is what we planned on and that was it.

Liz and Joe adopted a little girl and Liz told me she felt complete now. They were so happy to have a baby. They named her Anna.

Sarah had another little boy two years after Mike Jr. and they named him Daniel, which made Billy's dad feel special.

Jack and Izzy had a baby boy after Haley and they named him Jack, Jr.

Jesse and Maria had two children, one year apart. They had a boy first, which they named after my Dad, Samuel Jesse West. Then they had a little girl that they named Lisa Anne, after Maria's mom.

Buko and Barley are still alive and running both houses. They are good with the kids and they cuddle with them all the time.

Nick and Elise are both in school and doing very well. They are both well behaved. They love going to Connecticut for the summer months and they have friends there. They are the loves of our lives. I think we did ok as far as parenting goes. At least, our kids aren't complaining. They have everything they need and want.

My Billy still fuels my fire every single day. I love that man with all my heart and soul and he loves me back the same way. I still have the Teddy Bear that he gave me when I got promoted at work and it stays on our bed.

My mom and dad are doing well and they have lots of grandchildren now and also their kitties.

Billy's mom and dad are also doing well with lots of grandchildren and kitties. Gotta have those kitties. 🩶

Nick Ford is still in our hearts and we miss him terribly and we thank him all the time for all that he did for the both of us. He gave us more than an inheritance, he made us realize that you have to forgive and forget and that you never want to be alone with no one in your life. He is the reason we had our children.

Thanks Nick. We Love you! 

ACKNOWLEDGEMENT

THANK YOU CHRISSY FOR ALWAYS BEING THERE TO READ MY WORDS AND EDIT FOR ME.

I APPRECIATE IT MORE THAN YOU KNOW.